Somerset
FAMILIES

Robert Dunning

Somerset Books

First published in Great Britain in 2002

British Library Cataloguing-in-Publication Data
A CIP record for this title is available from the British Library

ISBN 0 86183 446 1

SOMERSET BOOKS
OFFICIAL PUBLISHER TO SOMERSET COUNTY COUNCIL

Halsgrove House
Lower Moor Way
Tiverton, Devon EX16 6SS
Tel: 01884 243242
Fax: 01884 243325
email sales@halsgrove.com
website www.halsgrove.com

Printed and bound in Great Britain by Bookcraft Ltd, Midsomer Norton

Contents

Introduction	5
Acland-Hood of Fairfield and Butleigh Wootton	9
Beaufort	14
Carew of Crowcombe	17
Cely-Trevilian of Midelney	21
Clark of Street	24
Dickinson of Kingweston	28
Elton of Clevedon Court	32
Fox of Tonedale	37
Gibbs of Tyntesfield	41
Gore-Langton of Newton St Loe and Hatch Park	44
Harbin of Newton Surmaville	48
Helyar of Coker Court and Poundisford Lodge	52
Hippisley-Coxe of Ston Easton	58
Hobhouse of Hadspen	63
Horner of Mells	67
Kemeys-Tynte of Halswell	70
Leir of Ditcheat	73
Luttrell of Dunster and East Quantoxhead	76
Lyte of Lytes Cary	81
Medlycott of Ven	86
Mohun of Dunster	90
Phelips of Montacute	94
Portman of Orchard	100
Poulett of Hinton St George	104

Seymour, Dukes of Somerset 110

Smyth of Ashton Court 118

Speke of Whitelackington, Dillington and Rowlands 121

Stawell of Cothelstone 129

Stuckey of Langport 134

Trevelyan of Nettlecombe 137

Vaughan-Lee of Dillington 141

Waldegrave of Chewton 145

Wills 149

Wyndham of Orchard 151

Envoi 156

Acknowledgements 158

Bibliography 159

Introduction

There was some pressure from the publisher to call this book *Great Somerset Families*, but the author resisted for two reasons: there was the difficult question of the definition of 'great' and 'Somerset', both of which might have been settled eventually, with a good deal of specious argument, to the satisfaction of both but to no one else; and there would have been the problem of rejection, particularly on the grounds of greatness. Let history make that judgement, but not a mere historian. Yet a judgement had to be made, or the book would have become too large. So this is a personal selection without a judgement of quality, made in part for reasons which will be clear in the text: families who have lived for long in the county and have made their mark in a wide variety of ways; families who have left behind enough materials from which to tell a continuous and coherent story; families who, in one way or another because of their social status or material possessions, have contributed significantly to life in the county. Three families have been included for a different reason; they bore the name Somerset in their titles.

It may, perhaps, be noticed that only about a quarter of the chosen families have their origins in Somerset. Neighbouring Devon gave birth to the Carews, Helyars, Gibbses, Leirs and Spekes; Dorset to the Harbins and Hoods; Cornwall to the Trevelyans; Gloucestershire to the Smyths; Oxfordshire to the Dickinsons. The commercial honeypot that was Bristol attracted not only the Dickinsons and the Smyths but also the Eltons from Herefordshire, the Hobhouses from West Somerset, the Phelipses from Wales, the Willses from Wiltshire. Marriage to an heiress brought a Wyndham from Norfolk; a landed inheritance a Waldegrave from Suffolk. Together, whatever their origins, those families formed and many still form a significant part of the history of the county, for they were quickly absorbed into its social structure through marriage, public service, generosity or sheer neighbourliness. This selection of such folk, individuals joined to each other in long lines of inheritance and families connected to each other by marriage and friendship or divided by political rivalry or personal antipathy, is a contribution to the social, political and commercial history of Somerset over more than half a millennium.

Public service is a common thread. The offices of justice of the peace, escheator, sheriff, deputy lieutenant or Lord-Lieutenant have come about at different periods of history in response to changing needs: local lay administration of justice, the financial and administrative needs of the Crown or local defence responses. In origin and for years afterwards there were serious demands attached to each, and each required of its holder a certain quality of leadership as well as an acknowledged social status. Politics might at any time promote or disqualify. To stand for Parliament similarly required a certain status and adequate finance for a county seat, though to be returned for a borough at an early date (as the Portmans were at Taunton) might be a doubtful and expensive privilege. But borough seats were not to be despised and the Luttrells, the Medlycotts, the Palmers and the Phelipses certainly did not despise them, for the growth of party politics gave every seat a greater value in both financial and political senses.

James Scott, Duke of Monmouth (executed 1685).

Lodge, ix

Thus county families in most periods were represented on their local bench of magistrates, dealing with day-to-day misdemeanours from the comfort of the Justice Room, with more serious offences at Quarter Sessions. At particular times, such as when the Church of England felt itself threatened by Nonconformists or landowners by Chartists, magistrates might take aggressive action. The head of each county family took his turn as sheriff and, given friendship or political alliance, served as a deputy lieutenant. That last office gave its holders the responsibility of raising the local militia at times of crisis, notably during Monmouth's Rebellion and when the country was threatened with invasion. The threat from Spain had been the catalyst for the creation of the office of Lord-Lieutenant and its holder was made responsible for the defence of the whole county. By that time the sheriff, the shire reeve, had become a mere figurehead, far removed from the essential and sole royal officer in the county he had been since Saxon times, though as returning officer at parliamentary elections, his partiality could be a valuable asset. Today sheriff and Lord-Lieutenant remain, Crown appointed, no longer the exclusive preserve of men; something much more than the harmless figureheads they were a century ago. They embody that concept of county whose loss was threatened when Somerset as well as other counties was dismembered to satisfy what was thought to be future need. That the present Lord-Lieutenant is the Queen's representative for a restored historic county is a recognition that the past cannot so lightly be cast aside.

Members of Parliament are now professionals and magistrates undergo intensive training; county and district councillors receive attendance allowances. Public service is not as voluntary as it once was. The introduction of statutory education and a national health service overtook the charitable foundations of Clarks and Foxes. That is not to imply that all magistrates were good and fair just because they were amateur, nor all MPs were bad just because they bribed their way into the House of Commons. It is to say that men (and now women) who were members of families portrayed in this book took on public service as part of their lifestyles; they saw it as a return for the privileges they enjoyed, it came with the territory. Whatever else they did, whom they married, whose side they took, where they travelled, how they behaved made them different from each other, made them individuals; as public servants they were united (most of the time), in the Middle Ages on royal commissions, then and later on the Bench, sometimes keenly following the government line, sometimes carefully sitting on the fence. And, for the historian, the more individualistic the better; the political division of the county between York and Lancaster, King and Parliament, Whig and Tory is the stuff of national history writ small.

The principal outward sign of family is the family seat and Somerset's country houses are a fine illustration of the way Somerset's families saw themselves. Little but the motte and the site are left of the home of the Mohuns at Dunster, less of course a home than an expression of original function as guardian of the West for the Conqueror. The present castle is the result of a victory of an ambitious architect over a modest squire. Montacute, still with its massive façade and turreted forecourt, is the result of another flamboyant architect entirely in tune with the ambitions of his client. Ven and Crowcombe are ambitions not realised and very dearly paid for. For the rest they are accretions, modest to begin with though added to as marriage alliance made possible or necessary or fashion (with or without adequate funds) dictated. The new wings at Ashton Court, Hinton St George and Brympton D'Evercy (none of them designed by Inigo Jones) directly resulted from marriages in the seventeenth century between Smyths, Pouletts and Sydenhams (and not, as was popularly supposed at Hinton, from a visit there by Queen Anne). The landscaped grounds of, say, Halswell, Mells, Ston Easton or Nettlecombe were natural responses to fashion by men who had no wish to be considered provincial and were, in fact, often in the vanguard.

Nettlecombe Court, the park, 1793; engraving by W. Angus after Smith.
SAS

Somerset was, of course, far from London, but not so far that the discerning could not recognise its possibilities; and Bristol's merchants in the eighteenth and nineteenth centuries had as much money as London's to invest in land and the social status and reponsibilities that went with it. The county produced its own entrepreneurs in the nineteenth century, but they were a more modest breed, content with more modest homes not far removed from the homes of those they employed. The attractions of the Somerset landscape, recognised by those with leisure at the turn of the twentieth century, have as yet rarely produced a Somerset family more than a century old; and the concept of retirement to such a 'promised land' is, by definition, a short-term phenomenon.

Acland-Hood of Fairfield and Butleigh Wootton

Sir Alexander Fuller-Acland-Hood (1853–1917), 4th Baronet of St Audries in Somerset, 6th Baronet of Hartington in Derbyshire and from 1911 1st Baron St Audries, was the descendant of more than the three families whose surnames he bore. His father had been baptised Alexander Bateman Periam Hood, and had taken the Bateman name and the Derbyshire baronetcy from his grandmother, the Periam name and the estate of Butleigh Wootton near Glastonbury from his great-grand-mother. The Fuller-Acland element came from his marriage to Isabel, only child of Sir Peregrine Fuller-Palmer-Acland, through whose Acland, Palmer and Verney ancestors the family could trace their own-ership of their home at Fairfield in Stogursey back to the end of the twelfth century.

The Hoods were from Mosterton, just across the Dorset border, and were either clergymen or sailors. Alexander was a favourite name in the family, Arthur and Samuel popular too. Of the three sons of the common ancestor Alexander Hood, the second was Arthur, rector of Dowlishwake, the third was Samuel, vicar of Butleigh. Samuel was father of those two remarkable admirals Samuel, Viscount Hood (died 1816) and Alexander, Viscount Bridport (died 1814). Alexander, the eldest brother, had a second son, Samuel, two of whose three sons, Alexander and Samuel, also distin-guished themselves at sea. Alexander, who served with Captain Cook, was killed aboard his ship the *Mars* in 1798, not many years after his marriage to Elizabeth, daughter and heir of John Periam of Butleigh. His brother Samuel, reaching the rank of vice-admiral, was created a baronet and served as MP for Westminster and Bridport. His title passed on his death in Madras (where he was in command of the India station) without chil-dren in 1814, under the terms of its creation, to his nephew Alexander, son of the gallant captain of the *Mars*. He served as MP for Somerset and died in 1851 leaving yet another Alexander as his heir and an Arthur, at least the fourth in six generations and an admiral, who in 1892 was created Baron Hood of Avalon and who died in 1901 at his home at Butleigh Wootton. Lord Hood's nephew Alexander (1819–92), the 4th Baronet, had served, unusually for the family, in the army, and had been a captain in the Royal Horse Guards. On his marriage to Isabel, the Acland heiress, in 1849 he

Samuel Hood, Viscount Hood, G.C.B., admiral (died 1816).

SAS

went to live at St Audries, an estate bought for Isabel by her father. He served as MP for West Somerset 1859–68.

Alexander, son of the last, also began his career in the army, serving with the Grenadiers in Egypt before going to Australia where he was on the staff of the Governor of Victoria between 1889 and 1891. He was returned to Parliament as a Conservative representing West Somerset, served in the Whips' Office as vice-chamberlain of the Royal Household under Lord Salisbury and as patronage secretary to the Treasury (Chief Whip) under Arthur Balfour. He was made a privy councillor in 1904. At home in Somerset he was a deputy lieutenant, a magistrate and a county alderman, all the offices of a man who took his local responsibilities seriously. He was created Baron St Audries in 1911 and died in 1917. His son Peregrine, the 2nd Baron, died unmarried in 1967 when the estate passed to his eldest niece Elizabeth Acland-Hood, then a teacher of mathematics in Kent. She married Sir Michael Gass, a retired colonial administrator, and after his death served as sheriff, on Somerset County Council and as chairman of Exmoor National Park Committee. In 1998 she was appointed Lord-Lieutenant, and somehow also found time to be South-West Regional Commissioner for English Heritage.

Right: *The Rt Hon Sir Alexander Acland-Hood, PC, MP, created Baron St Audries 1911 (died 1917).*

Mates

Below: *Sir Alexander Acland-Hood, Conservative Chief Whip, defends landowners against Liberal proposals, according to a cartoon in the* Daily Chronicle *1907.*

SAS

The Acland part of the family has even more complications and is linked with a house and estate as far back as the late twelfth century. Martin of Fairfield, taking his name from the delectable site where his descendant still lives, was succeeded as tenant by William Russell. William sired Ralph, and Ralph a daughter Margaret who brought the property to the Verneys. William Verney obtained licence in about 1473 to defend his house at Fairfield with a wall and seven round towers; other Verneys had been involved in dubious actions at Stogursey Castle in 1224, had interrupted divine service in Stogursey Priory Church in 1442, and had been fined in 1498 for support of Perkin Warbeck. Perhaps somewhat more respectable was that John Verney, a monk at Glastonbury by 1509 who was master of the novices in 1525, third Prior in the following year (a job for which he was criticised) and official in charge of the medary in 1539.

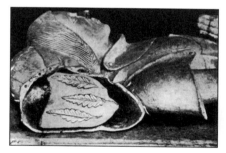

Monument to John Verney of Fairfield (died 1461), Stogursey church.

SASP lxx

Above: *Elizabeth Periam Acland Hood, Lady Gass, Lord-Lieutenant of Somerset (second from right), presents the Queen's Award for Enterprise to Yeo Valley Organics Ltd, 2001.*

Photograph Alain Lockyer

After Verneys, with the marriage of Elizabeth Verney to William Palmer towards the end of the sixteenth century, there followed four generations of Palmers, most of whom did their duty as MPs representing Bridgwater, Minehead or the county. Peregrine (died 1684) had been a soldier of fortune in the Swedish army under the great Gustavus Adolphus in his youth and had fought for the king in the Civil War. He and his eldest son Thomas (died 1681) were supporters of the court party, opposing the exclusion of James, Duke of York, from the succession for his Catholic opinions.

Colonel Nathaniel Palmer of Fairfield (died 1718).

SASP cxxxvi

Nathaniel, Thomas's younger brother, served in ten parliaments, five times for the county, three times for Bridgwater and twice for Minehead. He was one of the early supporters of William of Orange, but generally voted with the Tories. All three were well educated men with some legal training; Nathaniel commanded the county militia.

Elizabeth Palmer, sister of Thomas and Nathaniel, had married Sir John Wroth of Petherton Park, son of that intolerant Presbyterian who narrowly escaped being involved in the death of Charles I. Sir John's heir Thomas Wroth, was a minor in the care of his Palmer uncles. It was on Thomas's land at North Petherton that the famous Alfred Jewel was found in 1693 and it remained in Uncle Nathaniel Palmer's hands until his death in 1718. His son Thomas Palmer, fulfilling his wishes, handed it over to the University of Oxford. Thomas might well have been reluctant to see the cherished jewel leave Somerset, for his interests were antiquarian, and he left behind him an unfinished history of Somerset based on original sources, some of which are no longer to be found. He was also a politician, succeeding to his father's seat at Bridgwater which he occupied as a Tory with only a short break from 1715 until his death in 1735.

Thomas Palmer left his estate to his wife, a Wroth heiress whose money had evidently been of great use to him; and he left his body to be examined by various doctors who had been unable to find a cure for a complaint with which he had long been afflicted. After his wife's death in 1737 the estate ('what little is left') passed to his brother Peregrine, 'an honest plain man, much affected with the gout'. And from Peregrine in 1762 it came to his kinsman Arthur Acland. Arthur's son John stood for the nearby borough of Bridgwater in the election of 1780 with the support of the Poulett family, but lost. A petition on his behalf that the result had been unfairly achieved proved successful and he sat in the Commons from 1781 until 1784. He made little mark there but generally supported Pitt. One teller of votes described him as 'country gentleman, doubtful'. He did not stand again nor did he undertake much public service but instead improved Fairfield and its surroundings, creating a park in front and diverting roads to achieve greater privacy. He was created a baronet in 1818.

Peregrine Fuller-Palmer-Acland (the Fuller from his mother) served as sheriff in 1813–14 and succeeded his father as 2nd Baronet in 1831. In 1835 he bought the St Audries estate and from 1849 it was the home of his only daughter Isabel, wife from 1849 of Sir Alexander Bateman Periam Hood. Between then and 1870 the house was rebuilt in perhaps three phases, refaced and extended to provide 42 bedrooms, some for bachelors in a tower, the parish church was rebuilt and the park extended over the site of the former village, not only improving the surroundings of the house but providing much-needed employment for the tenants on the estate. Sir Peregrine died in 1871. The Acland-Hoods in the person of the 2nd Lord St Audries sold the house and land in 1925 and made Fairfield again their only home in West Somerset.

Above left: *St Audries, the Great Hall, 1891.*

W. L. Nichols, *The Quantocks and their Associations*, (2nd edn, 1891)

Above right: *Maud, Audrey and Alexander, children of Sir Alexander Acland-Hood, 1903.*

SAS

$\diamond\diamond\blacklozenge\diamond\diamond$

Beaufort

John Beaufort was the eldest of the three illegitimate sons of Edward III's son John of Gaunt by his mistress Catherine Swynford. His surname came from his father's castle in Champagne. He was born about 1371 and while still under twenty saw service on the unsuccessful crusade against the Moslems in North Africa led by the Duke of Bourbon. In 1394 he was in Lithuania fighting for the Teutonic Knights, and two years later he and his brothers and sister were declared legitimate. Parliament accepted the Pope's judgement on the matter and in 1397 John, who had been loyal to Richard II, was created Earl of Somerset with precedence immediately after the Earl Marshal. He was, after all, now a royal prince. Honours came thick and fast: Knight of the Garter, and on one and the same day Marquess of Dorset and Marquess of Somerset. He was summoned to the House of Lords by the former title until 1399 when he was degraded, the new king not caring for such a foreign title. Thereafter until his death he was Earl of Somerset. Degradation was not a punishment, though he had served Richard loyally and had been rewarded with the constableships of Wallingford and Dover, the command of two fleets, and the Lieutenancy of Aquitaine. He served Henry IV equally well, being Chamberlain of England, Captain of Calais and Constable of England. When there was a royal lady to be escorted somewhere, he seems to have been the man to do so; when the Count of St Pol beseiged a castle near Calais, he repulsed him; when the Steward of Hainault challenged him at a tournament in Smithfield, he knocked him from his horse. He died in the hospital of St Catherine-by-the-Tower on Palm Sunday 1410 and was buried in Canterbury Cathedral.

Henry Beaufort, John's eldest son, died at the age of seventeen in 1418, but he had already seen life, for he had accompanied Henry V on the Agincourt campaign three years earlier. His brother John therefore succeeded to the title. John's career began without much luck and ended rather worse. During the summer and autumn of 1420 he was at the siege of Melun but was taken prisoner at the disastrous defeat of Baugé in Anjou in 1421 and remained a prisoner for seventeen years. On his release (he was exchanged for a prisoner taken at Agincourt in 1415) he returned to the hopeless defence of the English lands in France, having a few successes and rather more failures. The government at home, seeing him as their only military hope, rewarded him in 1443 with the earldom of Kendal and the dukedom of Somerset 'for his nearness to the king in blood and good will to do the king service'. A year later he was home in disgrace and died very soon afterwards, some said by suicide. He had no male child and his dukedom and the earldom of Kendal became extinct. The earldom of Somerset devolved on his next and youngest brother Edmund.

Edmund, Earl and Marquess of Dorset, was by that time a seasoned warrior, taken prisoner with his brother at Baugé but not interned for so long. He may have gone on crusade against the Bohemian heretics with his uncle in 1429 and was certainly present at several engagements in France, for which he received his Dorset titles. He took his late brother's place as the overall commander of English forces in France and suffered a series of inevitable reverses against Charles VII including a disastrous and expensive surrender of Rouen in 1449 and of Caen in 1450. On his return home he was obviously associated with the failure of Henry VI's government by the opposition led by Richard, Duke of York, and when York was in power Beaufort found himself in the Tower of London for more than a year. His return to power precipitated the outbreak of war and at the first battle of St Albans in May 1455 he was killed.

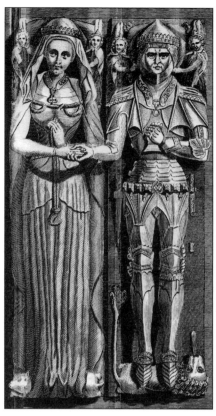

Tomb of John Beaufort, Duke of Somerset (died 1444) and his wife Margaret, Wimborne Minster.
J. Hutchins, *History of Dorset* (3rd edn. 1868), iii. opp. 216.

He died a very rich man, spoiled, people said, by extreme avarice, but others noted that he had been loyal to the Lancastrian line, the line of his grandfather John of Gaunt. Henry his son was in the same mould and, while still a minor, was fighting beside his father at St Albans and was wounded. There was soon a swagger about him as the Lancastrians retrieved power; his men fought the men of Coventry, he attended a Great Council with a troop of 200 horse, he took part in jousts at Smithfield and Greenwich. Soon he was effectively the king's only champion against the Yorkists and led the invasion of Queen Margaret's troops from France. He won the battle of Wakefield for the king in 1460 and the second battle of St Albans in 1461, but victory was short lived. After the dreadful defeat at Towton later in 1461 he fled to Scotland. He was, understandably enough, attainted and his titles forfeited, but after failure to secure French help for the Lancastrian cause, he made peace with Edward IV and was pardoned, his titles and lands being restored. At the end of 1463 he deserted the king for his old allegiance, led them to defeat at Hexham in 1464 and was there captured and beheaded. His pardon was, of course, reversed.

Henry Beaufort was unmarried but left an illegitimate son Charles who, when the Lancastrians came into their own again, was in 1514 created Earl of Worcester and became in due time the ancestor of the Dukes of Beaufort. There were also the Duke's two brothers, Edmund and John. Edmund would have been the next Duke of Somerset had Henry not been attainted, and both he and John were with Queen Margaret after Hexham. His fellow Lancastrians, ignoring the attainder, persisted in calling him Duke of Somerset. He commanded the centre at the battle of Barnet in April 1471 and the right at Tewkesbury less than a month later. John Beaufort, Edmund's brother, calling himself Marquess of Dorset, was killed in the fighting. Edmund, blaming the defeat on the Earl of Devon and Lord Wenlock, at least had the satisfaction of dashing out Wenlock's brains with his battle axe. After the battle he took refuge in the nearby abbey but two days later, probably tricked out of his refuge by a promise of pardon, he was beheaded in the town. The house of Beaufort and their Somerset title had come to an end.

Above: *Lady Margaret Beaufort (died 1509), mother and grandmother of kings; artist unknown.*

Lodge, i

Right: *Langport church. The Beaufort portcullis is on the east face of the tower.*

SAS

Except, of course, for that famous Lady Margaret, only daughter of John Beaufort, Duke of Somerset, who was born in May 1443. While still a child she was married to John de la Pole, Duke of Suffolk. She married secondly in 1455 Edmund Tudor, Earl of Richmond, by whom she had a son Henry, later Henry VII. Her third husband before 1464 was Henry Stafford (died 1471), and her fourth was Thomas Stanley, later Earl of Derby. Lady Margaret Beaufort, Countess of Richmond and Derby, the mother and grandmother of kings, bore titles far from Somerset. Yet of the estates which she inherited from her father and kept until her death in 1509 more were in Somerset than in any other county: Curry Rivel, Langport, Martock, Milborne Port and the hundreds of Abdick and Bulston. Her portcullis badge on the tower of Langport Church is a continuing reminder of a great lady.

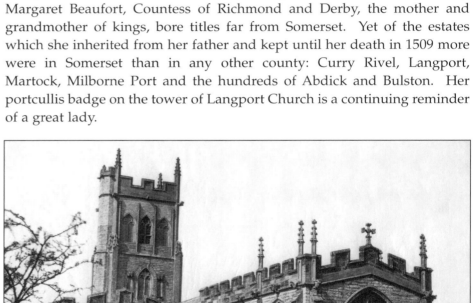

◇◇◆◇◇

Carew of Crowcombe

A marble monument in Camerton Church commemorates the death in 1721 of Thomas Carew, described as the son of Thomas Carew, merchant in London, who was the son of Thomas Carew of Studley in Devon, who was the son of Sir John Carew of Carew Castle in Pembrokeshire. In the north chancel chapel, built by a Carew in 1638, are the tombs of Sir John (said to have died 1640) and John (died 1685). An historian, writing at the end of the eighteenth century, certainly went along with the Carew Castle connection and spoke of a Sir William Carew whose son John married the Camerton heiress. So the Carews came to Somerset first by acquiring Camerton. But the family had Somerset connections before then, for Sir Edmund Carew of Mohun's Ottery in Devon served as Sheriff of Somerset in 1493–4 (and was killed at the battle of Thérouanne in 1514), and a Sir John Carew held the same office in 1506–7.

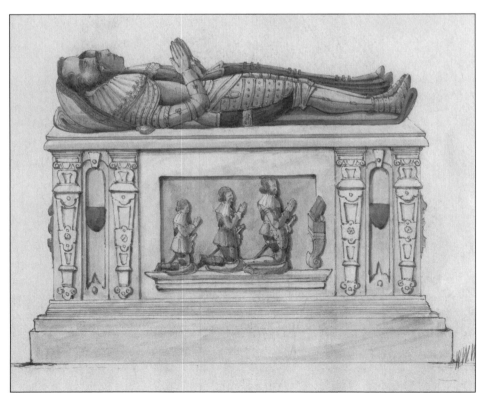

Monument of Sir John Carew (died 1637), Camerton church, 1844; wash drawing by W. W. Wheatley.

SAS

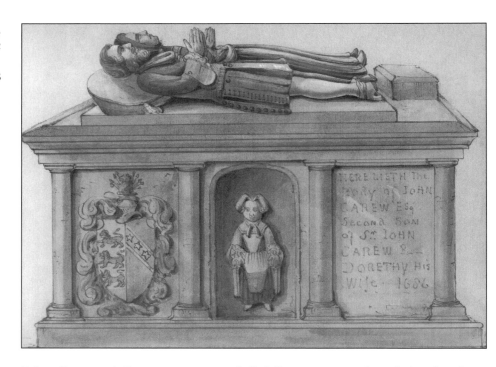

John Carew of Camerton was a dull fellow compared with his brothers George and Peter. Their father Sir William, of Mohun's Ottery in Luppitt, Devon, had married the daughter and heir of Sir Hugh Courtenay of Haccombe, near Newton Abbot, and Haccombe was the burial place of Carews from the time of Sir Nicholas in 1469. George Carew served twice as Sheriff of Devon and was elected for the county in 1529. He saw service in Calais, was made Vice-Admiral and on 19 July 1545 dined on board the *Great Harry* in Portsmouth harbour with the king, who gave him his chain with whistle pendant. Returning to his ship the *Mary Rose*, he ordered her sails hoisted and she immediately capsized. George's brother Sir Peter Carew, who was exiled for his part in the rebellion of Sir Thomas Wyatt against Queen Mary, rose to be Constable of the Tower of London and Lieutenant of the army in Ireland under Queen Elizabeth.

Thomas Carew, probably grandson of John, acquired a manor in Crowcombe by marrying Elizabeth, daughter of Hugh Biccombe. He was once thought to have been implicated in the Babington conspiracy. His elder son John, who was Sheriff of Somerset in 1633–4, had been appointed Sheriff of Pembrokeshire in 1632, a county which had recently become his home after Charles I granted him the entirely habitable castle at Carew. Sir John died in 1637 and was buried under an impressive tomb on the north side of the church of Carew Cheriton. A second tomb was made in his memorial chapel in Camerton Church by his son in 1640.

The family pedigree of both Camerton and Crowcombe branches has presented difficulties for historians, partly because John and Thomas seem to have been the only names used for several generations. John Carew of Crowcombe (died 1684) was sheriff in 1673–4; his cousin John of Camerton (died 1686) was sheriff 1678–9. Neither seem to have played any other prominent part in public affairs, though how both branches managed to keep a low profile during the Civil War and its aftermath is difficult to understand. Several bags of silver found in the family home during demolition, perhaps hidden during Monmouth's Rebellion, may suggest a strain of caution verging on the non-committal. The only member of the family to undertake any public service in the eighteenth century was Thomas Carew of Crowcombe who served as MP for Minehead 1739–47.

Horace Walpole called him 'a crazy zealot'. He was a Middle Temple lawyer who was returned by the Luttrell interest as a Tory and was immensely active, introducing bills including one which attempted to curb corrupt elections, another to prohibit 'a certain pernicious game called roulet or roly-poly' and another to prevent cursing and swearing by fines ranging from a shilling for labourers to five shillings for gentlemen and above. In 1755 he published (anonymously) a book entitled *An Historical Account of the Rights of Elections*, a useful work which he hoped would 'terrify candidates, agents, and electors from engaging in ... indirect practices' in parliamentary elections. The research involved in this enterprise, which he began when confined to his home because of illness in 1741 and resumed, again because of illness, in 1750, resulted in a collection of historical material which proved Carew a considerable antiquarian with very wide interests.

He was also an obsessive builder, pulling down the manor house at Crowcombe in 1724 almost as soon as he entered his inheritance. The new work was virtually completed in 1739, but not before one designer had been dismissed. The result is the finest house of its period in the county

Crowcombe Court, 1791; engraving by T. Bonnor.

J. Collinson, *History of Somerset* (1791)

south of Bath, but the cost was enormous, well over £4000, a sum only raised by the sale of six manors. Gardens, woodland and a park were also part of Carew's achievement, its progress told in a series of letters preserved by his successors. Among them are exchanges with his one-time friend and later bitter enemy Henry Lockett, the rector of Crowcombe, who for a long time was the unpaid bailiff of the estate.

Thomas Carew died in 1766 leaving two daughters. Elizabeth, who outlived her sister, married James Bernard and died in 1805. Her heir was Mary Carew, of the Camerton branch of the family, Elizabeth's first cousin once removed. She married in 1794 George Henry Warrington, who took the additional name Carew and served as sheriff in 1833–4. So the name Carew continued at Crowcombe (Camerton had been one of the manors sold by Thomas) until the death of Edmund George Carew in 1886 when the estate passed to his sister Ethel Mary, wife of the Hon. Robert Cranmer Trollope, the second son of Lord Kesteven. In 1934 Mrs Trollope was succeeded in turn by her grandsons A.J. (died 1942) and Thomas F. Trollope-Bellew. The present lord of the manor and representative of his line in Somerset is Mr A.H. Trollope-Bellew, who lives on one of the ancient farms on the estate.

◇◇◆◇◇

Cely-Trevilian of Midelney

T wo families again, closely associated with radical politics in the aftermath of the Civil War and thus ostracised for a time thereafter but uniting through marriage and inheritance. The Celys or Ceelys, according to family tradition, were in North Curry in the earlier sixteenth century and reached back from there (genealogically speaking) a further five generations to Bartram Ceely. The family clearly made its mark in the persons of the lawyer brothers William and Edward in Revolutionary Somerset in the 1650s after the victory of Parliament over the king. William was recorder of Bridgwater and was appointed a magistrate by the county's radical leader John Pyne – Pyne's deadly enemy John Ashe called him Pyne's 'slave and vassal' and 'a shuffling, beggarly lawyer'. In 1659, under the same influence, Edward Cely was a regular member of the county committee, removed from office as Pyne's influence waned but restored by Pyne to be a senior officer in the militia foot and a magistrate, probably until the Restoration. He served as sheriff in 1651–2. A third member of the family, another Edward, was described on his grave at Creech St Michael as a barrister at law and of Charlton, an estate which the

Creech St Michael church showing the Cely chapel on the south side, 1848. Wash drawing by W. W. Wheatley.

SAS

family had acquired through marriage. William Cely, grandson of Edward, succeeded as a minor and married a Trevilian daughter. They had at least six children including five sons of whom the fourth was named after his mother's brother John Trevilian and the fifth, William, was his uncle's heir and adopted his surname. William Cely-Trevilian died in 1774.

The Trevilians, according to Isaac Heard of the College of Heralds in 1815, were husbandmen of Midelney in Drayton in the reigns of Edward VI and Queen Elizabeth; and there was a family of husbandmen and weavers in Kingsbury, not far away, in the 1550s. It is from John of Kingsbury that the family traces its descent. An earlier Trevilian, Thomas, had in the company of the Abbot of Ford and others been lessee of a Ham stone quarry at Stoke sub Hamdon, again not far from Midelney, in 1474–5. Trevilians were said to have been tenants of Midelney in the later sixteenth century and Ralph Trevilian apparently acquired it in 1603. Richard, his heir, was one of two Trevilians who made their mark in the seventeenth century. The first was another Thomas who, when the town of Langport not far from Midelney was granted a charter of incorporation, became its first town clerk, a post he held for the next forty years. The second was Richard Trevilian, named in a lease of 1652 as lord of the manor of Midelney, who like the Cely brothers played a prominent part in county government in the 1640s and 1650s.

John Trevilian, son of Richard, was certainly a gentleman and was, according to his memorial in Drayton church, wise, trustworthy and honourable. He was recorder of Langport, the town's chief legal officer, from 1699 until his death in 1749, served as the first sheriff of the county under the Hanoverians in 1714–15 and was a county magistrate. John's heir was his nephew William Cely but he, having taken his uncle's name, failed to produce a son and at his death in 1774 his estate at Charlton passed to a nephew, William Southey, while Midelney went to his brother Maurice. Maurice thereupon applied to the Secretary of State for the Home Department for permission to take the name and arms of Trevilian in accordance with his uncle's will. A warrant to that effect passed the Signet, but a question arose about the arms. Apparently Sir John Trevelyan of Nettlecombe (died 1755) had taken John Trevilian to law for using the Trevelyan arms but had lost his case. Sir John's grandson, another John, had agreed with Maurice that there must be a common ancestry but subsequently changed his mind and refused to countenance the use of his arms. Sir John returned to the subject in 1815, making the point that the arms the Cely-Trevilians were then using were a new grant and in no way matched the antiquity of his own.

Maurice Cely-Trevilian lived in Bristol; the estate passed in 1781 to his sons John (died 1807) and William in turn. John abandoned the old family home, sold the herd of deer and ploughed up the park; William joined the army, reaching the rank of captain in the 10th Hussars, and in his turn held the family office of recorder of Langport until removed in 1795 for refusal to attend meetings. William's fourth son Maurice (1796–1861) served in the Peninsular war in the 14th Light Dragoons, retired as a brevet major, sat as a magistrate and at his death was living in a new house known as Midelney

Major Maurice Cely-Trevilian (died 1932).

SASP lxxviii

Place. By that time three of his five sons were dead, one drowned in Mexico. His heir was his second son, Edmund Brooke Cely-Trevilian (1833–1914), an Oxford graduate and a barrister, who married an American, Kate Sedley Fearing of New York. Edmund was a magistrate and a deputy lieutenant and was sheriff 1902–3.

Maurice Fearing Cely-Trevilian (1881–1932) was widely known throughout Somerset. He, like most of his class, had been to public school and went on to Oxford. He served in Gallipoli and Egypt in the First World War, was sheriff 1925–6, a magistrate and a deputy lieutenant. So much could be assumed. He was a leading churchman, a member of the diocesan conference and a governor of Woodard schools (as was his son after him). But he had a passion for rural affairs and a firm belief in the future revival of agriculture, and to that end he believed villagers should be made aware of the important part they would play. So he was a moving spirit in the formation and running of the Somerset Community Council, the local branch of the Folk Song and Dance Society and the British Legion; he trained village choirs, and wrote and directed pageants in many parts of the county. The writer of an obituary recalled his last speech when he called for the soldierly qualities of discipline, steadiness and comradeship needed when revival came. The present rural crisis has need of his like.

Richard Edwin Fearing Cely-Trevilian served in the Second World War and was sheriff in 1961–2. His son John now lives at the unique house that is Midelney Manor, once part of the holding of Muchelney Abbey and after its surrender one of the many estates of Protector Somerset, and ensures in his care for the house and estate a continuing home for his family.

Midelney Manor, 1955; photograph by Iris Hardwick.

SCC

Clark of Street

The medieval clerk was literate but not necessarily holy, a man who could read and write but not always in Holy Orders. The William Clerke who was on a jury with his neighbours to establish the boundaries of the abbot of Glastonbury's manor of Greinton in 1515 was probably the father of William Clerke the younger who held a small farm in the manor for which he paid a rent of 16s 1d and five hens. Mentioned in the same document was Thomas Clerke of Ashcott – uncle or cousin, who will ever be certain?

The younger William was chosen by William Day, Greinton's parson, to be one of the supervisors of his will in 1545. Another generation produced Dorothy aged eighty, Robert aged sixty and Joan, a widowed Clark daughter, who each occupied small farms in the parish. Yet another generation came to notice because they had found another enlightenment and were prepared to suffer to practise it, should government policy so decree.

Thus it was that in 1669 the house of John Clark was being used by a group of Quakers and that in 1670, when such activity was declared illegal and subversive, John Clark the elder was in trouble for keeping a conventicle. Three years later John and Joan Clark were found attending such a conventicle in Sutton Mallet and Clarks senior and junior offended again at Greinton. They were not dissuaded by a bullying and narrow-minded government, and in 1676–7 John the elder was fined £20 for continuing to allow his house to be used and John the younger 10s for being present.

But come the Glorious Revolution, the mind of government broadened. In 1689 the Clark house was licensed. Quakers on the Poldens were free to worship in their chosen way. That was not, of course, the end of trouble. John Clark was one of many who decided that, having been persecuted by the Church of England, he was not prepared to support it by paying church rates. He was in trouble in 1717 for making the point.

The records of Greinton are sadly lacking but in the eighteenth century a farm called Beavens was remembered by its earlier holders, Clark and Moor. In 1796, when land in King's Sedgemoor was being allotted, a free-

Cyrus Clark (died 1866).
M. McGarvie, *Book of Street* (1987)

holding called Bryant's held by Thomas and Joseph Clark was awarded some of the rich grassland. Thomas and Joseph were the sons of John Clark and his wife Jane, daughter of Thomas Bryant. One of Thomas's grandchildren married John Clothier and began an important and fruitful link between the two families. Joseph's two younger sons, Cyrus and James, gave up the farming activities of their ancestors.

From 1821 Cyrus worked as a woolstapler and fellmonger with Arthur Clothier at Arthur's tanyard in Middle Leigh, Street, and in 1825 moved to premises belonging to his father-in-law, a glover. There he set up a factory for making rugs. In 1833 he took his brother James into partnership and they added mops and chamois leathers to their production line. James had hitherto made slippers (later known as Brown Peters or Petersburghs) and shoe linings. From 1833 he made shoes. By 1851 huge progress had been made; in that year the brothers made £5000 from the sale of rugs and £21,000 from the sale of men's shoes. Their skill in dressing skins was extended from the staple diet of sheep to the skins of lion and tiger (lizard and leopard processing had to wait until about 1911).

James Clark (died 1906).
M. McGarvie, *Book of Street* (1987)

The firm only just avoided bankruptcy in the early 1870s and needed the injection of ideas and energy of a younger generation. James's sons William Stephens and Francis helped to lead the business as it began to make shoes for ladies and children which were sold throughout the Empire and the USA. In 1875 361,000 pairs brought in £76,000; in 1900 sales reached £143,000; in 1913 400,000 pairs were sold at home and a similar number abroad.

The family expanded and, making money, ploughed it back into the community. The Quaker ways of thought and practice they had inherited were as strong as ever. James Clark saw land as an investment, not for its own sake but for its future use. He bought the 328 acres of Street Farm in about 1888 and the Grange, the largest house in the parish, in 1890. They were later to be the site of a modern factory. William built a house called Millfield, towards the south-eastern edge of Street parish, in 1889; his son Roger acquired from the Clothiers a house called Whiteknights in 1900. Rather earlier, in the 1850s, the family had begun building 'superior cottages' for their workers, and from the 1880s until the beginning of the First World War architect-designed terraces and roads transformed the tiny agricultural village into an urban settlement, complete with Clark-financed and Clark-inspired schools (for art, cooking, housewifery and technical subjects as well as co-educational elementary and secondary establishments).

F. J. Clark (died 1938).
Clarks of Street, 1825-1950

William Stephens Clark (1839–1925), educated at Sidcot and York (with more than a smattering of chemistry from St Thomas's Hospital) was chairman of the family firm, C. & J. Clark, from 1904, chairman of Clark, Son & Morland (sheepskin rugs of Glastonbury) and chairman of Avalon Leatherboard. He was a magistrate from 1886, a county alderman when the office was first invented in 1894, and was particularly interested in education and the provision of public libraries. His brother Francis, his sons John Bright and Roger, his grandsons John Anthony Clark, William and

W. S. Clark (died 1925).
Clarks of Street, 1825-1950

Stephen Clark, and Peter Thompson, his nephews Hugh Clark and William Hinde, and others even unto the next generation, not to mention the many talented ladies of the family, continued and continue the family tradition of public service and charitable giving. It was typical that Francis Clark (died 1938), educated at Bootham School and University College, London, chairman of C. & J. Clark 1924–36 and a director of Friends' Provident Insurance, a magistrate and a Fellow of the Linnean Society, should in his time have also been a member of Street Urban District Council and captain of the Street Volunteer Fire Brigade. It was typical that in 1904 John Bright Clark (died 1933) should have been elected as county councillor for Street and that members of his extended family, T. Clothier and J.C. Morland, should have been returned respectively for Somerton and Glastonbury.

The Managing Staff, Clarks, c. 1925.
Clarks of Street, 1825-1950

Opposite: *Clarks' showcard c. 1924, designed by E McKnight Kauffer.*
Clarks of Street, 1825-1950

The business has changed. In 1881 about 1100 were employed, in 1901 1250, in 1928 1335, in 1935 1440. In 1985 Clarks shoes were manufactured worldwide by 23,000 workers producing 23 million pairs; but in Street the factory was closed in 1992, to be replaced by the popular retail centre named Clarks Village. A museum and archive tell the amazing story of the family and the buildings of Street are eloquent testimony to the finest traditions of what elsewhere might be called paternalism. Still standing, close to the former factory buildings, is the Meeting House which has always been at the heart of the family's faith and practice.

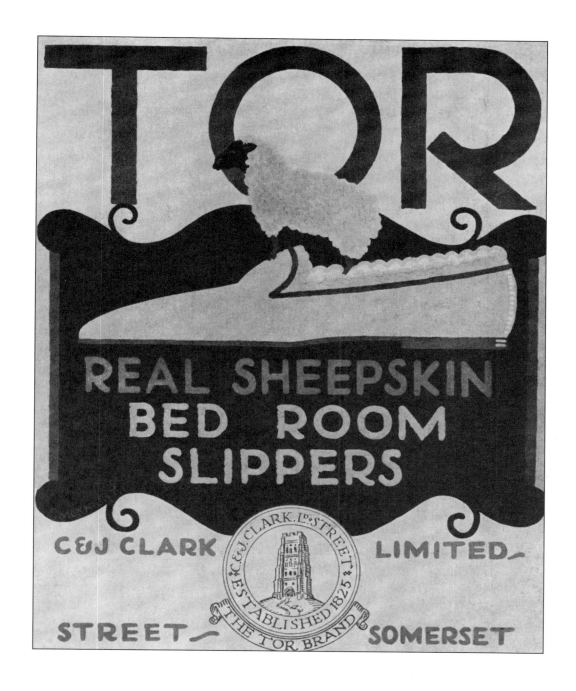

Dickinson of Kingweston

The Dickinsons were content to trace their family back to an Oxfordshire country clergyman of the earlier seventeenth century who, with his wife, had two enterprising sons. The elder, Edmund, educated at Eton and Oxford, was awarded the degree of Doctor of Medicine by his university in 1656 and in 1677 became a Fellow of the College of Physicians. He held the office of Physician-in-Ordinary to both Charles II and James II, dabbled in chemistry and wrote two books, one claiming to base a philosophy of life on the first five books of the Old Testament. Dr Dickinson died in 1707.

Edmund's younger brother Francis, from whom the family claimed descent, owned a sugar plantation in Barton, Jamaica (possibly held in association with other members of the family). Caleb, son of Francis, came back home and settled in Wiltshire although his business was based in Bristol where he was first apprenticed to a Bristol iron merchant, whose daughter he married. Like many Bristol merchants he invested in land outside the city, moving to Kingweston near Somerton in 1745.

Caleb's son, William, was educated at Edinburgh University and married into the Fuller family of Sussex, one of the leading planter families in Jamaica. In 1768, with whose influence is not known, he was returned to parliament for Great Marlow. He lost his seat in 1774 and had to wait until 1777 when the Fullers' influence gave him a seat at Rye. He lost that in 1790, the borough manager telling him to retire because 'the politics of the time' ran 'so contrary' to his own. By 1796, when he was well established at Kingweston, he was eventually returned as one of the members for Somerset, having wished to stand twice before.

During his career in the Commons he supported Lord North's government but was not entirely trusted; he was thought, like his son, to be a supporter of Pitt the younger. He had, perhaps understandably considering the source of much of his income, championed the West Indian opposition to the abolition of the slave trade in 1799. William Dickinson died in harness in 1806. His son, also William, educated at Westminster and Oxford and a barrister, was already an MP, having been elected for Ilchester in 1796 and for Lostwithiel in 1802. A firm supporter of Pitt, he offered the Prime

Minister his services and was rewarded with the office of Lord of the Admiralty which he held in the years 1804–6. In 1806 he stood for both Lostwithiel and Somerset, the first an insurance in case he did not win the county. He remained a county member until 1831, always independent but open to persuasion. In 1806 he was, as his father had been, opposed to the abolition of the slave trade, but in 1807 admitted he was impressed by the moderation of the abolition bill and did not oppose it.

His election for the county in 1806 was the first of seven successive and successful elections. He was returned unopposed in 1812 and headed the poll in 1818, although standing against a government candidate cost him £7000. He was an active magistrate, but needed some government support in order to become chairman of the county Quarter Sessions, for Sir John Cox Hippisley and Lord Porchester were strongly in favour of a Mr Acland. He was chairman from 1821 until 1835 and was also the last recorder of the borough of Glastonbury. A supporter of criminal law reform, he had become increasingly alarmed at 'the current wave of anarchy and rebellion' he sensed and took command of the East Somerset volunteers in June 1819. He was returned as senior county member in the elections of 1820, 1826 and 1830. William Dickinson died in Naples in 1837 after several months on the Continent. He had long been interested in Italy and had earlier joined the Dilettanti Society, hence his nickname Old Dilettante. His body was buried in Naples, but his heart was brought back to Kingweston.

Epergne presented 'by a large body of his constituents' to William Dickinson for his service in seven successive parliaments, 1833.

SAS

Francis Henry Dickinson, the next squire of Kingweston, tried politics first but found religion and antiquity more to his taste. He failed to obtain a seat in 1837 but for six years from 1841 he was Tory MP for West Somerset and in 1846 voted for the repeal of the Corn Laws. He was, as befitted his estate (it covered some 5000 acres and stretched from Kingweston as far south almost to Ilchester), chairman of the Somerton bench of magistrates and chairman of the board of Wells Asylum; he served as sheriff in 1853–4. The Church was to remain an abiding interest. He was described as mildly Evangelical, and a visit from one of his wife's relatives, the Revd Henry Manning, resulted in the foundation of Wells Theological College in 1840, a pioneer in the training of clergymen which Dickinson generously supported all his life. (Manning was responsible for the foundation of a similar college at Chichester but later left the Anglican fold, becoming a Roman Catholic Cardinal.) Dickinson entirely rebuilt Kingweston parish church, which was consecrated in 1855.

Antiquity was another of Francis Henry's constant enthusiasms, whether it was a possible Roman villa on his estate or something connected with the military history of the medieval period. He was a founder member of the Somerset Archaeological Society in 1849 and of the Somerset Record Society some forty years later, and he was said to have been 'for ever compiling fresh matter and drawing fresh conclusions'. He was never happier than writing pieces for the *Manchester Guardian*, and someone remembered him as 'a perfect walking dictionary of all kinds of knowledge, but he never bored'. He died in 1890 and his son and heir William, a shy man with a taste for painting in oils, travel, and living in London, died in 1914.

Francis Dickinson (died 1890).

SAS

William Francis Dickinson, Captain Dickinson as he was usually known, came upon his landed estate at the worst of times. It was encumbered by heavy mortgages, partly because of his grandfather's generosity, partly because of the fall in the value both of the Jamaican estate and of English farming land, partly (as his daughter declared) by the disinclination of the ninth and tenth generations to marry heiresses and the need to support unmarried sons and daughters. Farm sales were necessary in 1922 and 1930 before the debts were cleared. Earlier, of course, Captain Dickinson had served in the army, beginning in the 1st Battalion of the Royal Fusiliers and later in the Hampshire Regiment, a contrast to the young man who had found a taste for the artistic while at school at Bradfield, had enjoyed success on the amateur stage in London, and had trained as an architect under Gambier Parry.

Captain Dickinson's only son, Sergeant Pilot William Alexander Caleb, known to the family as Cay and trained at the Royal Agricultural College,

Cirencester, was killed in action in 1941. Kingweston House, a late-eighteenth-century building, somewhat grimly remodelled in about 1825 by William Wilkins, was also overtaken by war and became first the headquarters of a searchlight crew and later billets for WRENS attached to the Fleet Air Arm. Since 1946 it has been leased as a boarding house for Millfield School, Street, a function of which Captain Dickinson would surely have approved.

Kingweston House, 1828; J. P. Neale,
engraved T. Jeavons.

◇◇◆◇◇

Elton of Clevedon Court

lton origins lie in Ledbury in Herefordshire, but are for ever associated with Bristol where George and Isaac Elton, whose exact origins are still not known, settled in the seventeenth century. George was a master mason and a freeman of the city from 1639; Isaac lived on its eastern edge and took full advantage of what was going on there, such as the demolition of the castle and the clearance of Kingswood Forest, to become something of an expert in making roads, a builder of cottages, and a contractor with the city corporation for the clearance of household refuse. He is described in his will as a yeoman.

Isaac Elton died in 1695 and was followed by his eldest surviving son Abraham, a man at the very heart of Bristol's rise to be the second city in England; 'one of the greatest commercial magnates' with pioneering interests in brass and iron foundries, a principal share in weaving, glass-making and pottery, and – it went without saying in Bristol – in the shipping of the port. With Abraham as founder of the family fortunes, his descendants, inheriting some share of his genius, found themselves as members of the city corporation, as aldermen, sheriffs and mayors, MPs, owners of ships and mines and land.

Abraham began as a master mariner and by 1683 was a merchant, later trading in wool, wine and tobacco (he was caught growing some illegally), and being a partner in a copper works at Conham where imported copper was smelted using locally-dug coal. Calamine from the Mendips allowed brass to be made and Abraham himself bought up leases of land in many parts of the Bristol hinterland in his search for more coal, calamine and iron. An estate at Broadfield Down near Winford did not produce the hoped-for calamine but instead iron ore, millstone grit and red ochre, all of which he put to profitable use. And further afield he and his sons were partners in many ships trading from Bristol, some privateers, some probably slavers.

Abraham's sons Abraham, Isaac and Jacob, sounding like patriarchal partners though the family was at the time staunchly and soberly Presbyterian, assumed their father's mantle with enthusiasm. Abraham took over wool, wine and tobacco and was involved in glass making, and trading across the Atlantic and in the Mediterranean; Isaac was in sugar and silk; Jacob in copper, glass, sugar, gunpowder and, especially, privateers. Abraham, the father, was created a baronet in 1717, largely for finding the cost of men to serve in the army in Ulster. He was Whig MP for Bristol 1722–7 and died in the latter year, his estate popularly assessed at £100,000 and in reality worth a great deal more. His son and namesake by then had been MP for Taunton since 1724 (father bought Whitestaunton Manor in 1718 to give him a local interest) and in 1727 took over his father's Bristol seat. He already had a country house at Failand. A third-generation Abraham was a city alderman.

The second Abraham was a busy MP and in 1733 was given a hero's welcome in the city for his part in defeating Walpole's proposals for taxing wine and tobacco, commodities very dear to the hearts and pockets of Bristolians. He seems to have been less interested in business and was certainly less well-off than his father, partly because of the demands of his spendthrift son. His modest will mentioned glass and copper works and included the request that he be buried in Clevedon parish church, the first of the family to lie there. Son Abraham made a splendidly flamboyant mayor of Bristol, but it was all show and no substance. He was declared bankrupt in 1742, the year of his father's death, and fled to France leaving his more sober brother Abraham Isaac to pick up the pieces. The sale of lands at Glastonbury, Meare and Midsomer Norton and other places only realised £60,000 which was not enough.

Abraham Isaac was determined that the disgrace of his brother Abraham should be lived down. He trained as a barrister and returned to Bristol where, no doubt with the help of his uncle Jacob and other relatives, he was appointed town clerk in 1753 and held office for thirty years. He was a dominant figure in corporation business and judicial administration. As a good Elton, of course, he also served as both warden and master of the Merchant Venturers. Sir Abraham Isaac died in 1790, no doubt apprehensive about the future success being in the hands of his son and heir but at least secure in the knowledge that the Elton flair for business was alive in the hands of his cousins, sons of his uncle Jacob, who were trading from Bristol to Venice and Africa and America.

The Abraham who succeeded in 1790 was the 'tiresome and opinionated' young man who for a time returned to the nonconformity of his ancestors before, with some difficulty because of his enthusiasm, being ordained in the Church of England. Though an aggressive Evangelical and an authoritarian chairman of Somerset Quarter Sessions, he had enough Eltonian flair to realise that the popularity of the seaside could and should be turned to his advantage. The genteel resort of Clevedon was born with his full encouragement. What he certainly did not encourage was the marriage of his son and heir Charles to the daughter of a Presbyterian whose business prospects were not promising, but married they were; and in Charles the Clevedon branch of the family radically changed course, for Charles had been touched by the words of Coleridge and Wordsworth, fancied himself a poet and proved himself a scholar. A family marriage took them further into the literary sphere. Charles's sister Julia in 1807 became the wife of Henry Hallam (died 1859), son of the Dean of Bristol and the most widely read historian of his time before Macaulay. Their delicate and precocious son Arthur, a school friend of William Gladstone and a fellow Cambridge Apostle of Alfred Tennyson, died abroad in 1833.

New Clevedon, 1838, NE view from Church Hill by Lady Elton.

SCC

Arthur Hallam Elton, son of Sir Charles and named after that brilliant cousin, had run the Clevedon Court estate for his father and continued the development of the resort. He served as sheriff in 1857–8, was appointed a deputy lieutenant and in 1858 was elected MP for Bath as a Palmerstonian Liberal. The task did not suit him and he resigned a year later, returning to write his second novel, to enjoy the conversation of his tenant and neighbour Walter Bagehot, the economist, the friendship of the high-church historian E.A. Freeman, the creation of the model village of East Clevedon and the construction of Clevedon pier. He died in 1883 and was succeeded by Edmund, both his nephew and son-in-law, the son of Edmund William Elton whose behaviour had caused him to be sent to Italy to paint. His second marriage, to the daughter of an unfrocked priest, the bridegroom announced from Florence.

By now there were Eltons all over the world: a John Elton emigrated to Connecticut and was married there in 1671; a penurious Elton had been sent to Georgia as a 'worthy debtor' in 1750 and his descendants still live there; a promiscuous Elton a century later was sent to Pretoria to join the police force where one of his brothers joined him and the South African Eltons were born. Another brother went to India. And there were cousins in all sorts of places by 1883 including Charles Isaac (1839–1900) at Whitestaunton, 'the most erudite lawyer of his generation'. The baronet at

C. I. Elton, Q.C., of Whitestaunton (died 1900): cartoon by Spy in Vanity Fair, *1887 entitled 'Court Roll'.*

SAS

Sir Edmund H. Elton, Bt, JP (died 1920).

Mates

Clevedon Court, Sir Edmund, was a practical and kindly man, a member of the new Somerset County Council from 1894, chairman of Clevedon Urban District Council, sheriff in 1895 and a leading churchman. He was also interested in technology, inventing a bicycle brake, a dress guard clip for lady cyclists, a device to turn off street lights by means of gas pressure and, finally and triumphantly, 'Elton Ware', decorative art pottery which, incidentally, was taken up by Tiffany's in New York and was widely distributed in the United States.

The success of the pottery could not make up for the effects of the agricultural depression on the estate as a whole; and over-generous spending on extensions to All Saints' church in Clevedon and other causes was unwise. In 1919 eleven farms on the estate were sold, and when Sir Ambrose succeeded his father in 1920 it was not viable. Clevedon Court found itself suddenly without servants occupied by an unhappy man, and what was left of the model estate became little better than a slum. Sir Arthur succeeded his father in 1951. In him the artistic and the technological returned for he was a documentary film maker, specialising in work for the Shell Oil Company, and throughout his life (from forays with John Betjeman from Marlborough to the Railway Works at Swindon) he collected books and pamphlets on technology, wrote widely and was recognised as an authority on the subject. He died in 1973.

Clevedon Court was handed over to the National Trust in 1960 but Sir Charles Elton and his family still live there. Its history and the history of this remarkable family, based on the extensive family papers arranged by Sir Arthur in the 1950s were together the passion of his wife Margaret, a Canadian of Icelandic descent but in the years of her widowhood a formidable supporter of all things Eltonian and a worthy successor to the many gracious and talented ladies at Clevedon Court.

Clevedon Court, home of the Eltons since 1709.

SCC

Fox of Tonedale

From Wiltshire the Fox family moved to Catchfrench in East Cornwall and from there they spread to Par, Falmouth and Wadebridge. Edward Fox of Wadebridge, general merchant and Quaker, in 1745 married Anna, daughter of Thomas Were of Wellington, sergemaker. Their second son, named Thomas after his grandfather, joined the Wellington firm in 1768 after four years learning languages and making business contacts in western Europe and in 1772 became a partner. The capital of the firm by that time was £20,000.

The business, gradually depending more and more on the energies of Thomas Fox, involved the export of finished cloth through the Devon port of Topsham to Hamburg, Ostend, Bruges, Amsterdam and Rotterdam where it was widely used by the country folk of those parts. Weres were responsible for about half of Topsham's annual export trade of £50,000.

At the age of thirty-six Thomas Fox married Sarah Smith, daughter of Thomas Smith whose plain name and plain Quaker clothes and style of living belied the fact that he was a banker with a counting house in London's Lombard Street and a house in Stamford Hill. Trade was difficult in the later years of the eighteenth century. Distant cousins in the shipping business at Falmouth provided contacts with America but cash was often not forthcoming and Were and Company were less keen on payments in kind or in dollars. Then in the late 1780s Quaker contacts in London enabled Fox to get into the East India Company's trade, producing what were called 'long ells'.

In 1787, the year before the manufacture of long ells began, Thomas Fox began his bank, at first simply an adjunct of his cloth business but soon widely accepted, like that of Stuckeys, throughout the West Country. Fox Brothers was the name of the bank from 1844, Fox Brothers, Fowler and Co. from 1879, later Fox, Fowler and Co. It was the last private bank to issue its own bank notes and had over fifty branches and agencies when it was absorbed into Lloyds Bank in 1921.

Thomas Fox installed machinery in the factory in South Street, Wellington in 1791 but not until 1796 did he achieve full control as sole partner. Some three years later he built a new mill at Coldharbour near Uffculme, not far away across the Devon border. In 1803 he built a new factory on a site north of the town at Tonedale and four years later moved into a house beside it. Both buildings still remain and are now protected by law. In about 1805 the firm employed about 3600 workers.

By the turn of the century production was by no means confined to plain serges and long ells, at least when peace permitted. A book of samples of coloured and printed materials used to be among the family archives which probably included the 'plushes' made for markets in Portugal, red serges for waistcoats and printed serges for 'female dresses'. And then came 'flannels', which soon found their way to North and South America, Scandinavia and St Petersburg. Business with the East India Company was reduced when Fox realised that the material was to be used for cartridges.

Thomas Fox died in 1821 leaving his six sons as partners in Fox and Sons. Like their father they could not go to university, and until the repeal of the Test Act in 1828 were unable to hold the kind of public office which required an oath to uphold the Church of England. They could not, and had no wish to be, magistrates or to become involved in the military affairs as landowners worth much less assumed to be their right. But true to their philosophy of life they showed particular care for employees who produced by the mid-nineteenth century fancy tweeds as well as flannels. Profit sharing was introduced in 1863 and retirement pensions and other benefits in 1874, long before they were required by law, and the Tonedale factory had dining and recreational facilities and later perhaps the earliest day nursery.

And outside the factory sporting Foxes shared their enthusiasms and Quakerly Foxes their concerns for education and health. Harry Fox began a football club in 1874 (the pitch given by G.S. Fox), formed an Athletic Union in 1883 and a Harriers' Club in 1886 (his death in a climbing accident in the Caucasus in 1888 was a dreadful blow). Henry (died 1876) and

Thomas (1828–98) had built schools, C.H. Fox chaired the Wellington and District Technical Education Committee in the 1890s and later members of the family gave to the town Wellington Park in 1902, the Maternity Home in 1924 and an extension to the Cottage Hospital in 1935.

Like the Clarks, the Foxes faced the challenge of government demands for military supplies in their own inimitable way; not footwear in their case but legwear. Fox Brothers began producing puttees in the true shade of khaki for troops fighting in the Boer War, and during the First World War made 70,000 pairs. They continued to produce army clothing until the time of the Falklands War and did very well after the Second World War making cloth for the famous blue demob suits. The firm then had factories in Cullompton, Culmstock, Uffculme, Wiveliscombe and Weston super Mare as well as a subsidiary in Chipping Norton for the production of tweeds.

Puttees, 1991.

SCC

Again, like the Clarks, the Foxes were a family firm. They had been a public company since 1896 but still in 1947 the board was exclusively Foxes: Hugh, Howard, Julian, Lloyd, Harry and Tom. Two more members, David and Michael joined in 1950. By the early 1990s the business was operating in a different world and restructuring in the face of financial pressure resulted in what was effectively a takeover. Michael Fox alone remained, well over retirement age, to take responsibility when a government agency demanded the imposition of modern health standards which had long been beyond the resources of the business to implement.

Whatever the future of the factory which bears the Fox name, the town of Wellington has much to remember the family by in houses like Swallowfield, The Cleve (now an hotel), Foxdown, Oldway and Robin's Close – products of prosperity in the nineteenth century – and in characters like F. Hugh Fox, who played for England against Wales in 1890 and later served as President of the English Rugby Union and J. Howard Fox, alderman of Somerset County Council and a director of Lloyds Bank. The factory at Uffculme still offers the visitor a glimpse of a fascinating past.

J. H. Fox (died 1915).

SAS

Gibbs of Tyntesfield

The Gibbs family traces its origins to Devon, to Fenton in Dartington in the reign of Richard II and to Clyst St George in Henry VIII's reign where in 1560 John Gibbs bought an estate called Pytte. George Abraham Gibbs, who practised as a surgeon in Exeter, had three remarkable sons: Sir Vicary, the eldest, was twice attorney general; George (died 1818) was in business as a merchant in Bristol; Antony established a firm in Exeter in 1778 trading in serges with Spain, Portugal and Italy and from 1806 with Peru. The branch established in Lima was later to be the key, from the 1840s onwards, of the involvement of the house of Antony Gibbs and Co. in the import of Peruvian guano, 'the British farmers' favourite light fertiliser'. Antony Gibbs settled in London in 1808 and died in 1815, leaving his two sons, Henry (died 1842) and William in charge of what was still a small business. Thanks to guano and William Gibbs the

Tomb of William Gibbs (died 1875), monument in St Michaels' church, Exeter.

G. S. Masters, *Collections for a Parochial History of Wraxall* (1900)

firm expanded and from 1854 made profits of well over £100,000 in all but two years, achieving £251,772 in 1864.

William Gibbs retired from active business in about 1854 and was living in the sixteenth-century Charlton House in Wraxall. In 1862–4 he commissioned the architect John Norton to design Tyntesfield; the cost of £70,000 was no problem. His eldest son Antony succeeded him in 1875 after Exeter College, Oxford, and naturally went into the family business but sat on the Somerset bench of magistrates, was sheriff in 1888 and a deputy lieutenant for the county. His military service was as a major in the North Somerset Yeomanry Cavalry. Antony had three younger brothers, two of whom died unmarried in their twenties. The youngest, Henry Martin, bought Barrow Court, the Elizabethan manor house at Barrow Gurney created out of the nunnery on the site. Henry was a magistrate and was sheriff for the year 1897–8.

Charlton House, Wraxall, interior, from an old print.

G. S. Masters, *Collections for a Parochial History of Wraxall* (1900)

William Otter Gibbs, son of Henry, served in the First World War and became a major in the 10th Hussars. After the war he was colonel of the 5th Battalion of the Somerset Light Infantry T.A., was a magistrate for more than twenty years, sheriff in 1936–7 and a deputy lieutenant. In 1938 he served as aide de camp to King George VI. Soon after the Second World War he went to live in Scotland.

His cousin George Abraham Gibbs, son of Antony, was a soldier and politician. He was born at Charlton House in 1873 and after Eton and Oxford fought with the North Somerset Imperial Yeomanry in South Africa in 1900. He served with the regiment as colonel commanding both before and

during the war, but from 1906 combined his duties with those of Conservative MP for Bristol West. He served in the whips' office between 1924 and 1928, holding the office of Deputy Chief Whip and Treasurer of his Majesty's Household. He was sworn a member of the Privy Council in 1923 and in 1928 was created Baron Wraxall of Clyst St George, thus combining his possession of the manor of Wraxall with ownership of the family's estate at Pytte in Clyst. Lord Wraxall, an enthusiastic freemason, died in 1931. His obituary in the *Times* described him as 'an admirable example of that class of public-spirited country gentlemen who have for generations served this country in their homes and in Parliament'.

George Henry Gibbs, usually known as Henry, the eldest son of Antony, the merchant who died in 1815, settled at Aldenham near Elstree in Hertfordshire. His son Henry Hucks Gibbs, a director of the Bank of England for nearly fifty years and Governor 1875–7, was created Baron Aldenham in 1896. Henry's fourth son was created Baron Hunsdon in 1923 and was the grandfather of Antony Durant Gibbs, 3rd Baron Hunsdon and 5th Baron Aldenham (died 1986), who in retirement lived in the manor house at Rimpton and whose personal interest in his adopted home caused him, through the William Gibbs Trust, to sponsor a student to study its medieval history in depth. Such an interest was not unusual in the family. The 1st Baron Aldenham was a fellow of the Society of Antiquaries of London and his third son was Vicary Gibbs, merchant banker, barrister, politician and for more than forty years associated with the production of the *Complete Peerage*, a revised history of every titled family first produced by his uncle George Edward Cockayne, begun by himself in 1908. He continued his work on the project which he himself largely financed until his death in 1932.

G. A. Gibbs, MA, MP, JP, created Baron Wraxall 1928 (died 1931).

Mates

Gore-Langton of Newton St Loe and Hatch Park

The Gores made their name and fortune in London. Sir John was mayor in 1624-5 and his elder son and namesake became gentrified and settled in Hertfordshire. William, the younger son, exchanged a home in Morden in Surrey for Barrow Court in Barrow Gurney, for he had married a Wiltshire lady and the West Country called. Edward Gore, one of William's grandsons, was also of Barrow Court, the house which grew out of a Benedictine nunnery, and married Arabella, the sister and heir of Sir John Smyth of nearby Ashton Court.

Two of their grandchildren made marks in different ways. One, Charles of Barrow, was a clergyman and served (perhaps not very actively) as vicar of Henbury, just outside Bristol on the Gloucestershire side, and was the father of Montague, the first of the family for some time to undertake public office. He was MP for Barnstaple for a time and served as sheriff of Somerset 1852–3.

William, Charles's elder brother, married very well indeed. His mother was an heiress from Kiddington in Oxfordshire and his links there encouraged him to join the Oxfordshire militia, of which he became Lt Colonel in 1782. When he married a year later, his wife brought him back to Somerset for she was Bridget, only daughter and heiress of Joseph Langton, the grandson of a successful Bristol Merchant Venturer, who had acquired the old St Loe estate at Newton St Loe and had built on it in 1762–5 a fine new mansion. Stiff Leadbetter had probably been his architect and Capability Brown had certainly designed the magnificent surrounding park.

It was only right that William Gore should, in consequence of his good fortune, become William Gore Langton. He was less successful in politics. When Earl Poulett encouraged him to stand for a Somerset county seat in 1784 he was hissed off the platform. He did not try again until after his first wife's death, and when in 1795 he stood again he was returned unopposed; William Dickinson, the only other possible candidate, coming in the following year instead. The war with revolutionary France actually proved more interesting for a time and in 1798 he took up with the Oxfordshire militia again as their colonel.

Newton Park, Newton St Loe, 1791;
engraving by T. Bonnor.
J. Collinson, *History of Somerset* (1791)

In parliament his record was odd; he helped to defeat the Addington government in 1804 but found himself unable to afford to stand in 1806, threatening to leave Somerset altogether. For four years he sat as a Whig for the rotten Cornish borough of Tregony although he did not always vote as expected. He gained the Somerset county seat again in 1812 without spending any money and usually opposed the government, but he lost it to Sir Thomas Buckler Lethbridge in 1820. He sat again for Somerset in 1831 and was returned in the first reformed parliament for Somerset East, which he represented until his death in 1847.

Gore-Langton's sons epitomised their class and their time. One died in Ceylon, two served in the army (one at Waterloo); William Henry swopped country for town, a Somerset magistrate and a deputy lieutenant, he lived in Clifton and served as MP for Bristol 1852–65. His eldest son William lived at Combe Hay, not far from his father's house at Newton Park, but died in 1828. His marriage to the only child of the rich Henry Powell Collins of Hatch Park, Hatch Beauchamp, brought another mansion and another name into the family.

William Henry Powell Gore-Langton (1824–73) inherited two parks, Hatch from his mother, Newton from his grandfather. He served as might have been expected – as county magistrate, deputy lieutenant and MP (for West Somerset 1851–9, 1863–8). He paid for the restoration of Newton parish church and added a new aisle in 1857. His marriage to Ann, only daughter of the 2nd Duke of Buckingham and Chandos, brought him near a title and names in abundance, for the 2nd Duke was none other than Richard Plantagenet Temple-Nugent-Brydges-Chandos-Grenville, Duke of Buckingham and Chandos, Marquess of Buckingham, Marquess of Chandos, Earl Temple of Stowe, Earl Nugent, Viscount Cobham, Baron Cobham and Lord Kinloss. The 2nd Duke died in 1861 a ruined man, bankrupt after heavy borrowing and heavy spending. He left less than £200. His much more respectable son the 3rd Duke (he left nearly £80,000) had no sons, so at his death in 1889 his titles were either lost or shared around the family. The dukedom and marquessates became extinct and the earldom of Temple of Stowe passed to his nephew William Stephen Gore-Langton.

The new Earl, an early member of Somerset County Council and formerly an MP for Mid Somerset, added the name Temple to his own in 1892 and died in 1902. His son the 5th Earl served in the Somerset Light Infantry and was succeeded on his death in 1940 by his nephew Chandos Granville Temple-Gore-Langton, 6th Earl Temple, who sold the family home and estate at Newton Park to the Duchy of Cornwall. The 8th Earl has homes in Hampshire and Orkney; two of his children have West-Country connections.

The Rt Hon Algernon William Stephen Temple-Gore-Langton, 5th Earl Temple, JP (died 1940).

Mates

Henry Powell Gore-Langton, brother of the Duke of Buckingham's heir, made his home at Hatch Park and served as Colonel of the 3rd Battalion of the Somerset Light Infantry. His third son and heir Hubert Edwin was a naval commander and holder of the DSO awarded in 1918. He was still one of the two principal landowners in Hatch Beauchamp in 1939 but his home, Hatch Park, was destroyed by fire in 1942. All that survives of the former Collins estate is the charming Buttle's Lodge of about 1835 and the fine entrance gates.

H. P. Gore-Langton of Hatch Park (died 1913), brother of the Duke of Buckingham's heir.

SCC

◇◇◆◇◇

Harbin of Newton Surmaville

Robert Harbin (died 1621), builder of Newton Surmaville.

Robert Harbin was a Dorset man who succeeded in that age of conspicuous success, the sixteenth century. His family probably came from Milton Abbas, in his early years still dominated by its great Benedictine abbey. From there he moved to Blandford where he was known as a mercer and evidently invested in land in Stalbridge and finally in Gillingham and was described as a gentleman. There is no doubt that he was a gentleman and that he was also a scholar, for his portrait, at the advanced age of ninety-three, painted two years before his death, shows him holding a small book in one hand and a pair of eyeglasses in the other. The starched ruff and tasselled cap suggest a man conscious of his appearance and just a little frivolous.

He came to Somerset in 1608 at the age of eighty-two, the purchaser of the ancient estate at Newton Surmaville, divided from Dorset only by the River Yeo. Its previous owner had been deeply in debt, owing Sir Walter Raleigh as much as £600. On his new estate Robert Harbin built a house, probably within the next four years, in which his descendants have lived ever since. There are still traces of an earlier building in the service range but the old was successfully swept away. A plaster overmantel in one of the principal rooms bears the family arms, granted to Robert by that great antiquarian William Camden in his capacity as Clarenceux King of Arms. The world could now see, if it did not know already, that the Harbins were gentry.

Robert Harbin, son of John and grandson of Robert the builder, succeeded to Newton in 1639 and was soon much involved in what came to be the Civil War, at first espousing the cause of Parliament and taking part in its victory near his home at the battle of Babylon Hill in 1642. He was one of several committee men who went over to the king and received a royal pardon early in 1644, a matter of some satisfaction to his son John, already a strong royalist. Robert's erstwhile friends turned on him when they came to power and he lost his estates for what was called delinquency in 1647 but he secured possession for a fine and an Act of Oblivion passed by the Rump Parliament put the past behind him. His son, however, had to obtain a further Act in order to sell much of his land to pay debts.

The position of Newton Surmaville, almost straddling the Somerset-Dorset border, seems to have been an ideal situation for a family whose modest aspirations are illustrated by marriages to equally modest people living within a very few miles of Newton. William Harbin, son of royalist John, married into such a family, the Wyndhams of Trent. The Wyndhams had had a fierce and sweet hour when they had sheltered Charles II after the battle of Worcester, but now they were unable to pay their daughter's dowry and portraits, plate and two embroidered caps (said to have been worn by the king) passed into Harbin hands and are still at Newton. William Harbin died in 1705 and was succeeded by his son Wyndham, who married a Swayne of Tarrant Gunville in Dorset and named his son and heir Swayne. Family piety caused Wyndham to put up a memorial in Yeovil church to his ancestors going back to his great-great-grandfather John. Why builder Robert was omitted is a mystery.

Swayne Harbin died in 1780, the only member of his family to hold public office when he served as sheriff of Dorset in 1747–8. A second Wyndham Harbin, grandson of the first, died a bachelor in 1837. His mother Barbara continued to live at Newton until 1809 and in Wyndham's absence (he lived in Hampshire) the estate was under the care of his brother William, a Sherborne solicitor who had married a Phelips daughter from Montacute. George Harbin, William's elder son, eventually succeeded and did much to modernise the family home. He had no children, and on the death of his widow in 1898 the estate passed to his nephew Henry, son of his clergyman brother Edward, who had seen service in the East India Company's naval forces and in the army in the Somerset Rifle Volunteers and the Somerset Light Infantry.

On the colonel's death no more suitable heir could have been found in Newton's long life but his nephew Edward Harbin Bates. He was the

Newton Surmaville, Yeovil; photograph by A. F. Kersting.

eldest son of Thomas Bates of Heddon-on-the-Wall, Northumberland, and his mother was the daughter of the Revd Edwin Harbin, sometime rector of Kingweston and East Lydford. He himself had been educated at Eton and Cambridge, served his first curacy in Leicestershire and his second in East Somerset in the benefice of Cucklington and Stoke Trister. In 1898 he became rector of Puckington, a cure he held until inheriting Newton in 1909. With surely no reluctance he thereupon took his uncle's name in addition to his own.

Prebendary Edward Harbin Bates-Harbin (died 1918).

SAS

In his comparatively short life (he died in 1918 aged fifty-six) he became a master of Somerset history and it was entirely appropriate that he should have been appointed to write the parish histories for the projected *Victoria County History* – the sum of 250 guineas was offered but in the event he was diverted to produce the text of Domesday Book for the county and other related material – a scholarly undertaking which has stood the test of time but for which he received a meagre £59 7s 9d. His output as both researcher and editor was little short of phenomenal; he was an original member of the Somerset Record Society, an honorary secretary, president and trustee of the Somerset Archaeological and Natural History Society, closely associated with *Somerset and Dorset Notes and Queries*. Sir Henry Maxwell Lyte recalled his 'spring of ready wit and joyousness which came bubbling up in letters and in conversations about the distant past no less than about the ordinary affairs of life' and declared that in his death the county had 'lost a very notable antiquary'.

Prebendary Bates-Harbin left a widow Hilda, one of the daughters of Sir Theodore Fry of Cricket St Thomas, and a young daughter Sophia, whose second name, Wyndham, recalls that illustrious and romantic link with her distant ancestors. Sophia, emulating her builder-ancestor, still lives in the family home; and in her deep knowledge of Somerset history, some of it published by the Somerset Archaeological Society, she follows both her father and the great Dr George Harbin, non-juror and friend of Bishop Thomas Ken and accomplished scholar.

Helyar of Coker Court and Poundisford Lodge

L ike the Harbins, the Helyars came to Somerset as buyers of an ancient estate, only just a few years after Robert Harbin bought Newton Surmaville. The similarity continued, for the purchaser of the estate at East Coker, Dr William Helyar, archdeacon of Barnstaple in the diocese of Exeter and a canon of Exeter Cathedral, was a comparatively old man of fifty-seven years, and he lived in his new house until the year in which the first Civil War came to an end, reaching the age of eighty-six. There was another curious connection between the two. Harbin had bought Newton because its previous owner owed large sums of money. One of his creditors was Sir Walter Raleigh, and Raleigh was instrumental in Helyar's preferment as archdeacon.

Coker Court, East Coker: the north entrance front; photograph by A. F. Kersting.

There all similarity ended, for Dr Helyar was content with the house he had bought. His neighbour Thomas Gerard declared that he repaired the building and added some new parts, but the only things to be identified now are the fine stone screen at the service end of the hall, two fireplaces and a plaster ceiling, all in the fashion of the time. He himself by inclination was conservative if his politics are any indication.

The Helyars were by very distant origin craftsmen, helliers being makers of stone-tiled roofs. The family, perhaps remembering Archdeacon William, liked to think that Richard Helyar who died in 1446 was a forebear, for had he not been in turn archdeacon of Barnstaple and archdeacon of Cornwall, at the same time a canon of Crediton and Glasney, Cardinham and Bosham and evidently a trusted colleague of the good bishop Edmund Lacy of Exeter?

The College of Heralds would have none of this connection, but began the family pedigree with a William Helyar of St Budeaux who in 1555 married Alice Veel. Their son entered Hart Hall, Oxford, in 1571 at the age of eighteen. He was given the living of Bickleigh near Tiverton in 1577 and later acquired Dunchideock, Charleton, Heavitree and North Tawton, holding some of them at the same time. He was said to have been a chaplain to Queen Elizabeth, a canon of Exeter from 1596 and archdeacon of Barnstaple from 1605. At some time he was also a fellow of Chelsea College. In 1607 he was granted a coat of arms, like the Harbins, by the great William Camden, evidently a preliminary to investment in land, and in 1616 he bought the manor of Coker from Sir Robert Phelips.

Archdeacon Helyar may now have seen himself as a country gentleman but he remained a loyal priest of the Church of England and was prepared, even at a great age, to put up a fight against the fanatical Independents who threatened his cathedral. It is said that the altarpiece there in the 1640s had been beautified and adorned 'at his procurement, at least, if not his prime charge'; enemies even suggested it had been done to curry favour with Archbishop Laud. The response of those who would desecrate the place the archdeacon considered holy was to drag him from his bed, beat him, throw mud at him and imprison him in a disused ship until he paid a fine and a forced loan which together amounted to £1000. His death soon afterwards was hardly surprising. Among his legacies was a row of almshouses which still stand at the end of the tree-lined drive to Coker Court.

Archdeacon Helyar outlived his son but his grandson, also William, was made of the same stuff as his grandfather. After a spell at Exeter College, Oxford, and Lincoln's Inn (for a gentleman needed a little culture and a smattering of the law if he was to run an estate and act as a magistrate), he raised a troop of horse for Charles I but had the misfortune to be forced to surrender twice during the Civil War and his fine amounted to £1522. Somehow, it is said, he still managed to send money to the exiled Charles II (in consequence of which the family silver became pewter) and when the king came into his own again, so did Colonel Helyar. He served as sheriff of Somerset in 1661–2, was a captain in Colonel Berkeley's regiment of militia, hunted down seditious conventicles, was active against the Duke of Monmouth as a deputy lieutenant and died at the age of seventy-five in 1697 leaving his manor of East Coker, an estate in Devon and the lease of a Jamaican sugar plantation to his son, another William. The family considered one of their most precious possessions to be a miniature of the martyred Charles I.

William, the heir, who like his father had been to Oxford and Lincoln's Inn, married a Wyndham as his first wife and as his second a daughter of William Harbin of Newton Surmaville, so the connection between the two families was renewed. Some time before that he had in 1688 signed the declaration of support for the Prince of Orange but as MP for Ilchester in the Convention Parliament of 1689–90 he had voted to agree with the Lords that the throne was not vacant. He gave up his seat in 1690 and showed no more political inclination until 1715 although he was a magistrate from 1691, a captain of militia by 1697 and served as a deputy lieutenant from 1700 and as sheriff 1700—2. In 1715 he successfully captured one of the seats for the county as a Tory and sat until 1722, voting against the government in all but one of the recorded divisions. The only member of his family to be an MP, he did not stand again. He died in 1742, to be followed by yet another William.

Coker Court: the eighteenth-century east front; photograph by A. F. Kersting.

That William Helyar, grandson of the last, succeeded to Coker and through his mother, a Wiltshire Goddard, to land in Wiltshire and Dorset. Thus during the years 1766 to 1770 he could afford to spend a good deal of money rebuilding the east wing of his house in the Classical style of the day

and inserting a floor in the medieval great hall to provide more rooms. He took his turn as sheriff in 1764–5 and died in 1783 having fathered six sons and four daughters. The eldest son was, of course, a William, who married Elizabeth Hawker, heiress of Poundisford. He was a local magistrate but never sheriff or anything so flamboyant. His younger brothers led much more exciting lives: Edward went to sea; Charles was a soldier fighting in the American War of Independence and dying at the battle of Cowpens in 1781. A map of Charleston showing the dispositions of Cornwallis's troops was returned to Coker with the rest of his belongings.

William Helyar of Coker Court (died 1783), with a drawing of his extension to his home, by Thomas Beach.

Simon Heneage, Esq

The next William (1778–1841) was a magistrate in Somerset, Wiltshire and Devon and was sheriff of Somerset in 1829–30. His son, christened William Hawker (1812–80), amazingly broke the family mould both in his name and in his marriage, not to the daughter of some family of local gentry but of the Marquis de Resnel, a colonel formerly in the service of Louis XVIII. Horace Augustus Helyar, MA, JP, DL (1853–93), a diplomat who saw service in Madrid, The Hague, Washington, St Petersburg and Munich, succeeded in 1880 and died young but still outlived his only son William Annesley Weston Helyar, so his heir was his daughter Dorothy Margaret. In 1902 she was married to Major Godfrey Clement Walker Heneage, DSO, MVO, Grenadier Guards, owner of an estate at Compton Bassett, Wiltshire.

The Heneage pedigree could be easily traced back to Sir Robert Heneage (died 1536), father of Sir Thomas of Copt Hall in Essex, Privy Councillor and Chancellor of the Duchy of Lancaster under Queen Elizabeth, and of Michael, Keeper of the Records in the Tower of London. Mrs Walker Heneage remained in possession of Coker Court until her death in 1947 when the family sold its contents and left. Her son David followed family tradition, marrying Joan Cely-Trevilian, a member of a family which has lived in Somerset since the sixteenth century. Their son Simon lives in the county still.

So, too, do the Helyars of Poundisford, who look back to Charles John (1796–1858), the fifth son of William Helyar (1745–1820), who inherited the estate from his mother. Magistrates for three generations, the family have had more than a fair share of tragedy for Colonel C.W.H. Helyar of the 3rd Hussars was killed in action in South Africa in 1900 and his second son Commander K.C. Helyar, DSO (who succeeded his elder brother in 1910) was killed in 1940. Commander Helyar's son still lives in Poundisford Lodge.

Opposite: Colonel C. W. H. Helyar of Poundisford (killed 1900).
R. Dunning, *Pitminster* (2000)

Poundisford Lodge, Pitminster, 1870.
R. Dunning, *Pitminster* (2000)

Hippisley-Coxe of Ston Easton

A monument once gracing the walls of the charming little church at Cameley claimed to trace 'the respectable family of the Hippisleys' back to a Sir John Hippisley in the time of Edward I. More authentically they were in the early sixteenth century up-and-coming Mendip farmers, though at least two were less than well behaved, accused in 1533 of helping to breach the dam creating Emborough Pool and thus depriving the Carthusian monks of Witham of their fish. William Hippisley of Midsomer Norton, perhaps their father, had died some years before, holding land there and at Emborough, Farrington Gurney, Stratton and Chilcompton and leaving to his son John a sheep farm. Probably that John was tenant of the farm of Ston Easton which the owners, the canons of Bruton, had no wish to farm themselves; and when the abbey was dissolved John and his sons John and William were the sitting tenants. John and a partner were able to raise the sum of over £557 to buy that farm and land in Compton Dando, Bruton and Wincanton.

John, the son, was a lawyer as well as a landowner, educated in the Middle Temple, of which he later became a bencher. He was returned as MP for Bridport in Queen Elizabeth's first parliament and for Wells (as well as for Wootton Bassett) in 1563. He was Wells' legal advisor and a freeman of the city, but more importantly was recorder of Bristol, and he is considered to have been 'perhaps the most successful country practitioner of his time, … whose interest … was far more widely spread than even that of the Pophams'. He and his wife invested in more land, including the manor of Cameley, where they made their home, but also in many other parishes across Mendip.

John Hippisley died at the age of forty at the height of his powers and three Johns followed in succession as head of the family, all three lawyers, or rather all three educated at one or other of the inns of court and able, therefore, to be active and well-informed magistrates. John, the third of the trio, succeeded at only nine years old in 1614 and thus did not come into his inheritance until 1626. Not many years afterwards he was charged with a heavy sum of money by a royal commission because he had not attended Charles I's coronation to receive the degree of knighthood, an unpleasant method of raising cash which hardly endeared John to the Crown. His answer, of course, was that he had been a minor at the time and thus ineligible for knighthood. Perhaps that experience helped him to choose which side he took during the Civil War. He certainly took his office as magistrate seriously from the 1630s, no matter which party was in power, but by 1642 with his brother Richard and Thomas Hippisley, perhaps a cousin, he stood with the Horners (his grandmother was a Horner), Robert Harbin and his father-in-law John Preston among others in favour of Parliament.

Parliamentarian John was followed in 1664 by his two sons, John (died 1665) and Richard (died 1672) and Richard by his son Preston. Preston died in 1723 leaving an only daughter Margaret, wife of John Coxe, for a very short time MP for Milborne Port. Their only son John Hippisley Coxe, so runs his monument in Ston Easton church, often refused 'a public station in Parliament' for 'his inclination [was] early fixed to a country residence'. He was educated at Westminster and Christchurch, Oxford, and was a freeman of the city of Bath. Like many of his contemporaries he was bent on leaving his mark on the landscape by converting the rather old-fashioned gabled manor house of his ancestors at Ston Easton into a Palladian mansion with a garden and park to match. Richard his son, succeeding his father in 1769, had also been educated at Westminster and Oxford and married a lady 'born in the affluence of fortune'. That was perhaps just as well, for when he stood with Sir Charles Kemeys Tynte as a candidate for one of the two

Ston Easton Park, 1791; engraving by T. Bonnor after E. Garvey.

J. Collinson, *History of Somerset* (1791)

Somerset county seats in 1768 success cost him over £2600. He sat for sixteen years and was described by an astute observer as 'a young man of very quick parts'. He did not marry and for two years before his death in 1786 he was in the care of his brothers because of his lunacy. He had, however, finished the work which his father had started on the family mansion. It was left to his brother Henry to alter the park according to the fashion of the times and to the design of Humphrey Repton.

Henry Hippisley married twice but produced no children, his second wife, Elizabeth Anne Horner, being described as 'of masculine character, having at some time or other expressed a wish to be made a justice of the peace'; more like an early example of women's lib. After his death she clearly ruled the household at Ston Easton with some firmness, but among her innovations was a plunge bath. Henry Hippisley was an officer in the Somerset militia, served as sheriff in the year of the beginning of the French Revolution and was elected a county MP in 1792 in spite of opposition from the government. Thereafter he usually voted against them. His career was short for he died in 1795, leaving his estates to his nephew Henry, son of his sister Margaret by her husband and extremely distant cousin John Hippisley of Stow on the Wold. His widow, evidently the marrying kind after all, then married Sir John Cox Hippisley, an altogether remarkable man, son of a Bristol haberdasher. Ston Easton remained her home until her death in 1843.

John Hippisley of Stow was not then a landowner but its incumbent, for he was a clergyman who had first held the family living at Cricket St Thomas, from 1765 that of Stow and from 1767 also Stanton Fitzwarren in Wiltshire. He became a landowner in 1769 when a cousin left him the family estate at Lambourn in Berkshire. Richard, the elder surviving son of John and Margaret, inherited considerable estates in Devon including Shobroke Park and took the additional name of Tuckfield. Henry, the younger, another clergyman, went to live at Lambourn and a few years later bought more land a few miles away at Sparsholt. His three sons shared between them the family estates of Ston Easton and Lambourn and the rectory of Stow. The eldest, John, educated at Rugby and Oxford, became the archetypal country gentleman, serving as magistrate, sheriff and deputy lieutenant for Somerset. He wrote a tract about the state of the Church of England in 1851 and was a fellow both of the Royal Society and of the Royal Astronomical Society, and was a pioneer photographer.

The scientific interests of John Hippisley were inherited by two sons and a grandson. Clare Robert (1842–1918) had his own observatory in Bath; Richard Lionel (1853–1936) was a mathematician and military engineer who was Director of Telegraphs during the Boer War from whose organisation sprang the Royal Corps of Signals. Richard John Bayntun Hippisley, grandson of John, was like Richard Lionel an engineer and he was also a wireless specialist who put his knowledge at the disposal of both military and naval intelligence during the First World War, before which he had been commissioned in both services. He was also a founder member of both the Royal Automobile and the Royal Aeronautical clubs, for he was a

C. R. Hippisley (died 1918).

Mates

pioneer in both motor vehicles and aircraft. At the same time he remained more than a little suspicious of the domestic uses of both electricity and telephone. Yet he served his county well as magistrate, high sheriff, deputy lieutenant and, from 1931 to 1949, county alderman.

Lt Col and Cdr R. J. B. Hippisley, C.B.E. (died 1956).

Mates

R.J.B. Hippisley died in 1956 and by that date was no longer living in the mansion but in a more modest and manageable house in the village. The mansion was sold shortly afterwards and its very existence was threatened. Now, restored to the splendour envisaged by its creators as a fine hotel, the early-nineteenth-century retainers of Lady Hippisley Coxe look on its guests from a gilded frame. The family marches on: John Preston Hippisley was still claiming in 1972 to be lord of the manors of Ston Easton, Ashwick and Cameley and patron of the living of Cameley and Temple Cloud; one son was then an insurance broker living in Scotland, with children; another was a university lecturer in the U.S.A. There are still Hippisleys in Somerset, and the personal representatives of J.P. Hippisley still have a share in the patronage of Clutton with Cameley.

Retainers at Ston East Park; artist unknown.

Hobhouse of Hadspen

Hobhouses have been traced to Milverton in the later fourteenth century, to Holcombe Rogus, just over the Devon border, in the sixteenth and the seventeenth centuries, to Langford Budville and to St Decumans, all essentially West Somerset but none certainly connected with one another until they settled in Minehead. There John Hobhouse was clearly associated with the port by 1675 as a mariner and wheelwright and at his death in 1711 he left three sons, two of whom, Benjamin (1682–1749) and Isaac (1685–1763), saw better prospects in the great port further up the Channel and moved to Bristol.

Isaac Hobhouse and Company had become a force in maritime business by the early 1720s. In 1723 Isaac was wholesaler, factor and shipowner with interests in Boston and the West Indies in the trade in which most of Bristol prospered. Already by 1729 he had managed eleven voyages and was later to be a partner in a Somerset copper company. He died unmarried, but his brother's family included five sons who, like him, were members of the city's Society of Merchant Venturers.

City merchants achieving prosperity saw land as a safer investment than the high risks of maritime trade in a period when the changing fortunes of war vied with the uncertainties of weather to disrupt the safe return of valuable cargoes. Yet Hobhouses were never simply emergent country gentry; in four generations two were created barons, one a baronet and eight were prominent enough either in national or local government or in politics to merit inclusion in the *Dictionary of National Biography*.

Henry Hobhouse, grandson of Benjamin, settled at Hadspen in Somerset in 1785 and his descendants are still at home there. Benjamin, another grandson, acquired through his first marriage a share in a Bath bank ('very rich and sturdy' someone called him) and was a lawyer and moderately radical MP, serving as a minister through his friendship with Henry Addington. He was created a baronet in 1812 and made his home in Wiltshire. His sons included the much more radical John Cam Hobhouse, Baron Broughton de Gyfford, friend of Byron, government minister under Melbourne and Russell; and Benjamin, whose promise was cut short at Waterloo.

Left: *Sir Benjamin Hobhouse, Bt (died 1831); engraving by J. Cochran after J.Jackson.*

Right: *John Cam Hobhouse, Baron Broughton (died 1869), portrayed in 1819.*

A combination of scholarship and brilliance in government was the key to the career of the second Henry Hobhouse of Hadspen. His father had come with means, had tinkered a little with the house, had modestly increased the estate and had sent his son Henry to Eton and Oxford. The younger Henry continued the modest expansion of the estate into Shepton Montague and by 1849 he owned 715 acres in Pitcombe. But Henry Hobhouse was not principally a country gentleman; indeed, the estate was not large enough for such a claim and he chose a career in government and became a barrister. For some years he was legal adviser to government departments until in 1817 he was appointed permanent under-secretary for the Home Department. In 1826 he began his remarkable twenty-eight-year spell as Keeper of the State Papers, in effect the chief state archivist. In that capacity he was responsible for making the records of the reign of Henry VIII available to scholars. He was made a Privy Councillor in 1828.

He had, unsurprisingly, remarkable children including Arthur, judge and educationalist, who was created Baron Hobhouse in 1885 in order to try appeal cases in the House of Lords. Edmund was bishop of Nelson, New Zealand (1858-65) and assistant in the diocese of Lichfield 1869–81. He was also one of the founders of Culham College, who in retirement in Wells was a founder of the Somerset Record Society, a society which still exists to publish the historical records of the county and he contributed the first and the fourth volume.

Edmund Hobhouse, Bishop of Nelson, New Zealand (died 1904).

SAS

Henry Hobhouse, grandson of the state archivist, was a pioneer too; for him it was the emergent sphere of local government. In 1885 he was elected as Liberal MP for East Somerset and served from the next year until 1906 as a Liberal Unionist. He was a member of the Privy Council from 1902 and was chairman of Somerset County Council (1904–24). He was also for many years a Church Commissioner and member of the Church Assembly and was especially interested in education (the family coat of arms is among those of other benefactors in the Council Chamber at Bristol University of which he was Pro-Chancellor) and agriculture. One son, Sir Arthur Hobhouse, briefly a Liberal MP (1923–4), was a member of Somerset County Council for thirty-four years (chairman 1940–47) and chairman of the influential National Parks Committee (1945–7) which led to the creation of national parks. Another, Sir John, made his name in shipping in Liverpool, was a great supporter of the city's university and came to retire to West Monkton, serving as the first chairman of the South-West Region Museums Service. A cousin, Sir Reginald, the 5th Baronet, made his home at Pondmead, Oakhill, was a member of Somerset County Council (1919–47) and served as sheriff (1932–3).

The Rt Hon Henry Hobhouse (died 1937); portrait by C. Hall Neale.

SASP lxxxiii

More recent members of the family have made their names in different spheres, one as a philosopher and journalist, another in gardening, another as an architectural historian and conservationist and yet another, combining local government with his former career as an international journalist, has written challenging books one of which, *Seeds of Change*, became for a time almost cult reading among students in the United States.

Cover of Seeds of Change *by Henry Hobhouse (1985).*

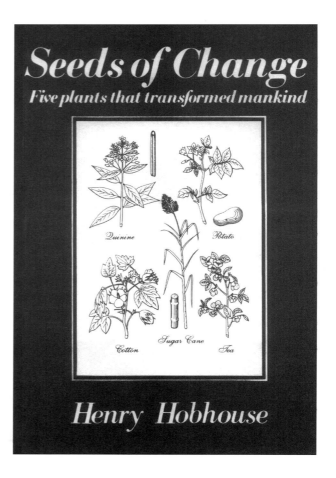

◇◇◆◇◇

Horner of Mells

Historians usually marvel how John Horner, although bailiff of Glastonbury Abbey's manor of Mells, could possibly have found the huge sum of £1831 19s ½d. to pay to the Crown for the former abbey manors of Mells, Leigh on Mendip and Nunney. A 'plum', certainly, but hints have been dropped that the transaction may not have been entirely above suspicion and that the piecrust hid a doubtfully-acquired deed of title.

But two John Horners, one called the elder and one of Stoke St Michael, were, at least in the 1530s, the years covered by the account books of the international cloth dealer Sir Thomas Kytson, deeply involved in the cloth business. The first was called cloth broker and cloth worker and dealt not only in white (undyed) English cloth but also in Bruges satin and sarcenet and imported woad. John of Stoke produced kersies for the Flemish market and also bought in woad. There was money in cloth, worth investing in land.

The transition to country gentleman had come by 1563 when John Horner, then living in the manor house at Cloford, was chosen to be sheriff (and again in 1572). It was clear, too, when his sons Thomas and Maurice sat in parliament in 1584, one for the county, one for Taunton, and when his daughter married Bishop John Still. Thomas sat again in 1586, was a magistrate and in 1606–7 sheriff.

Sir John Horner, son of Thomas, made his home at Mells and his name as one of the moderate leaders of the Parliamentary cause in the county during the Civil War, raising troops in 1642, defending Bristol in 1643, losing his estates but being obliged to be hospitable to the king at Mells in 1644. Appointed sheriff by Parliament in 1644–6, he again raised troops to take Bristol and in 1645 conducted elections which, somewhat deviously, kept out most of the radicals and ensured that his son George sat for the county. He himself sat in the Parliament of 1654–5 as one of the eleven members for Somerset and died in 1659.

George Horner was a Presbyterian but not the leader his father had been – 'a known neuter, if not worse' said the radicals. By the time his father

Thomas Strangways Horner.
Earl of Oxford and Asquith

died he had come round to supporting the king's return, sat in parliament and was knighted. Thus the Horners took their place again in the county Establishment. Sir George's son, also George, trained as a lawyer, led his local militia but was not whiggish enough for the extremists although he declared in favour of the Prince of Orange in 1688. His son Thomas, who succeeded him in 1707, sat for the county as a Tory and was twice unseated at Wells within a year. So close was he to the Tory leader Sir William Wyndham that he was nearly gaoled for suspected Jacobite sympathies.

Then came a family tragedy. Thomas married Susanna, heiress with her sister to the Strangways estates in Somerset and Dorset. When the sister died in 1729 Thomas and his wife inherited the whole estate including Melbury and Thomas added Strangways to his name. The couple had one surviving child, Elizabeth. Without Thomas's knowledge Susanna arranged a clandestine marriage in Guernsey between Elizabeth and Stephen Fox, brother of her particular friend Henry Fox (Susanna's 'extreme love' for Henry is mentioned in family papers). Thomas objected because of the age of the bride and the politics of the bridegroom, and evidently never forgave Elizabeth.

The magistrate Thomas Horner, 1790.
Earl of Oxford and Asquith

Opposite: *Thomas Strangways Fortescue Horner (1807-43) (seated) and J. S. H. Horner (1810-74).*
Earl of Oxford and Asquith

Thomas's brother John and his successors continued to do their duty as magistrates and sheriffs and married into families of local politicians like the Hippisleys and the Dickinsons but never again sat in parliament. Thomas Horner, 1737-1804, was a worthy magistrate whose notebooks are rare survivals and whose passion was for his landscaped garden at Mells Park and perhaps the largest hothouses in the country. His eldest grandson Thomas died in 1843 before succeeding, and the estate passed to the next brother John, already rector of the parish and for thirty years its squire too. John Francis Fortescue Horner, who succeeded in 1874, was in turn magistrate, sheriff and deputy lieutenant and from 1895 to 1907 served the Crown as Commissioner of Woods and Forests, for which post he was highly qualified as owner of a unique collection of pines, and for which he was made KCVO.

Sir John had the great misfortune to be the last surviving male Horner. His younger son Mark died of scarlet fever at the age of sixteen in 1908; his elder, Edward, who 'embodied the grace and gifts of his generation to a quite exceptional degree', was killed at Cambrai in 1917. The blow was the greater because in the previous year Raymond Asquith, son of the prime minister and husband of one of Sir John's daughters, had died at the Somme.

Sir John Horner died in 1927. The tragedies of the family are commemorated both in church and village by distinguished works of art commissioned by Lady Horner. For many years the manor house next to the church was home to Mrs Raymond Asquith. It has for long now been the home of her son Julian Edward George, who succeeded his grandfather as 2nd Earl of Oxford and Asquith in 1928.

Kemeys-Tynte of Halswell

The Tyntes thought they came from Newland in Gloucestershire in the thirteenth century; they were certainly in Wraxall in Somerset by 1327 and stayed there until Edward Tynte married a Gorges daughter and before 1619 bought the manor of Chelvey. Edward's son John managed rather better and moved to Goathurst, his wife's home in West Somerset, for he married Jane, the sole heiress of Hugh Halswell, the clergyman successor of a long line of Halswells dating back to the thirteenth century.

Monumental brass to John Tynte (died 1616) in Wraxall church.

A. B. Connor, *Monumental Brasses in Somerset* (1970), plate lx

Before moving west, however, John Tynte, Colonel Tynte as he was usually called, had men to recruit and battles to fight on behalf of his king. Not until 1656 was he to be trusted by the republican government; back in 1645 men of his cavalry regiment, led by a younger member of his family in his absence, had gone on the rampage in Axbridge, Berrow, Lympsham and South Brent; he had been imprisoned in Taunton, and fined. But he had visited Charles II in Jersey in 1649 and that was perhaps remembered when at the Restoration he was proposed for the Order of the Royal Oak. He was an obvious candidate for election as MP for Bridgwater in 1661 for the Halswells had influence there.

Tynte's father-in-law outlived him and his son, tactfully named Halswell, actually succeeded in 1672. Two years later, probably in recognition of his father's services to the Crown, he was made a baronet. Like his father he represented Bridgwater in parliament, but his political opinions were something of a mystery. He was more successful as a builder, turning the house of his ancestors into a grand mansion, probably with the help of William Taylor, a man who evidently advised Sir William Portman at Orchard at the same time.

John Tynte, the 2nd Baronet, married a Welsh heiress, Jane Kemeys of Cefn Mably, but the Kemeys name was not adopted, curiously, until the Tynte name was, strictly speaking, lost. Sir John's three sons, Halswell, John and Charles all died without children, although Charles (died 1785) left one of the finest landscaped gardens in the country and was the first of his family to represent Somerset in parliament. His heir at his death was his niece Jane, wife of John Johnson, not only a colonel in the 1st Foot Guards but a

Halswell Park, 1791; engraving by T. Bonnor.

J. Collinson, *History of Somerset* (1791)

member of the Household of George, Prince of Wales. Lady Tynte, Sir Charles's widow, occupied Halswell until her death in 1798, enjoying the splendid garden and especially the hothouses where she grew her favourite melons.

The new occupants were the Johnsons, who changed their surname to Kemeys-Tynte in appreciation of their good fortune. Their son Charles Kemeys-Tynte (1778–1860) sat in parliament for some years representing Bridgwater and wore the uniform of a colonel in the West Somerset Yeomanry. Perhaps his greatest coup was to persuade the Committee of Privileges of the House of Lords that he was a co-heir to the ancient barony of Wharton. His son, Charles John, declaring his Welsh as well as his English interests, served as colonel of the Royal Glamorgan Light Infantry as well as MP for West Somerset and later for Bridgwater.

Eldest son and grandson died within a few years of each other, both magistrates and officers in the local militia, and it fell to Charles Theodore Halswell Kemeys-Tynte, a modest magistrate in both Somerset and Monmouthshire and a former junior officer in the Royal Monmouthshire Regiment of Engineers, to find himself in the middle of the Great War Baron Wharton, a member of the House of Lords.

The barony had been created in 1544 as a reward for the loyal service given to the Crown by Thomas Wharton, victor of the battle of Solway Moss

C. T. H. Kemeys-Tynte, Baron Wharton (died 1934).

Mates

against the invading Scots. Thomas, the 5th Baron, a great supporter of the Glorious Revolution of 1689 and a leader of the Whigs in the House of Lords, was in 1706 created Earl of Wharton and, when the Hanoverians came, Marquess of Wharton, Malmesbury and Catherlough. His son Philip had a curious career; he was created Duke of Northumberland by James, the Old Pretender, and Duke of Wharton by George I while still under age, fought against the British at Gibraltar in 1727 and ended his life in exile in Spain in 1731 at the age of thirty-one, penniless, in disgrace and without children.

The new Baron Wharton, the 7th, died in 1934 having survived the devasting fire at Halswell House in 1923 in which family paintings by Vandyke and Gainsborough were destroyed. His son, the 8th Baron, served in the Royal Air Force in the Second World War and died childless in 1969 leaving an only sister who had two daughters. In 1990 the barony, again in abeyance, was determined in favour of the elder, Myrtle Olive Felix, wife of Henry Macleod Robertson. Lady Wharton was an active member of the House of Lords and served as a Vice President of the RSPCA. She died in 2000.

$$\diamond\diamond\blacklozenge\diamond\diamond$$

Leir of Ditcheat

T he Leirs are said by their historian, Michael McGarvie, to have been dull and rather unadventurous, but more than one enriched himself and his successors with marriage to a lady of property and in each of eight generations provided at least one clergyman, usually and remarkably the eldest and not a younger son, who occupied one or other (and sometimes both) of the family's two livings, Charlton Musgrove and Ditcheat. It was as if they regarded a rectory as other families regarded a manor.

So the Leirs were clerical gentry. They made rather outrageous claims for their origins, but the fact that they were not certain how to spell their surname made conclusions difficult. Eventually they plumped for Devon as their home for 'many centuries' but Richard Layer, Lyer or Leir came to Somerset when Francis Glanville of Tavistock appointed him rector of Charlton Musgrove in 1717. That Richard stayed at Charlton until his death in 1654 when he was succeeded by his son Thomas, although he was more Anglican than Presbyterian and was not properly accepted until 1660 when minds had changed.

Thomas was officially appointed by George Taylor, a member of his mother's family, but in the following year all was secured legally when he bought five-sixths of the advowson (the right to present the rector) from the Glanville trustees and in 1667 the remaining sixth. Thus the rectory of Charlton was available to any member of the family ready to take Holy Orders. But Thomas had two sons, both clergymen, so in 1695 he did a deal with the patron of Ditcheat, Edmund Dawe; in return for £100 Dawe promised to appoint Thomas Leir's eldest son, also Thomas, when the fifty-nine-year-old rector should die. Young Thomas was then up at Wadham and was told in no uncertain terms that to find the £100 his father had had to sell some land; he was therefore not to spend too much himself. His brother was there too.

In the event the wait was not for long. The rector died in 1699 leaving a young and well-off widow, Mary; young Thomas promptly married her and settled with her at Ditcheat where he was rector until his death in 1730.

Brother William succeeded their father at Charlton Musgrove when the old man died at ninety-three.

In 1727 Thomas of Ditcheat was able, with the help of his wife's money, to buy the advowson of Ditcheat, which cost over £1000. Their only son, Thomas of course, in turn became a clergyman and took over Ditcheat when his father died in 1730. He was, in that generation, the only male, so he took on Charlton Musgrove when his uncle William died in 1743. Ten years earlier he had married a daughter of Paul Methuen, a rich Wiltshire clothier. Two of their sons became insane; their eldest, yet another Thomas, became a clergyman. In 1781 he succeeded to both his father's rectories.

That Thomas married the daughter of a prosperous Warminster grocer and their eldest son, who clearly could not manage money, had no inclination for the Church either. Another son took to the law, but there were two, William and Paul, who were determined to continue the clerical line. In due course, when their father died in 1812, William went to Ditcheat and Paul to Charlton.

The Revd C. E. Leir (died 1924), rector of Charlton Musgrove and later of Ditcheat.

Mates

William had two clergyman sons and two clergyman grandsons, ensuring that members of the family were rectors of Charlton until 1914 and of Ditcheat until 1946. William himself decided to retire at the age of ninety-three and was succeeded at Ditcheat by his elder son William Marriott Leir, then rector of West Bagborough. William Marriott had a passion for hunting, and still in his eighties rode with the Blackmore Vale and with the Devon and Somerset staghounds, having a hunting box at Porlock Weir. At his death in 1891 he was remembered for his kindness and consideration as a landlord and the kindliness and serenity of his disposition, 'in the truest sense of the word a "fine old English gentleman"'.

It was perhaps no surprise that the eldest son chose the army for a career; his father, after all, had served with the North Somerset Yeomanry during the Bristol riots of 1832. Richard Langford was fond of country pursuits like his father and was keen on his family's history. But the army called and he was successful, rising to be a major-general. He rose socially, too, for his wife, a widow, was the daughter and heir of Lord Dorchester. The new Mrs Leir was as aware as her husband of the importance of family and required her spouse to add her maiden name, Carleton, to his. Eventually she persuaded Lord Salisbury to persuade the Queen that she should become Lady Dorchester. The general was, no doubt, delighted.

The Revd L. R. M. Leir (died 1914), rector of Charlton Musgrove 1886-1914.

Mates

Opposite: *General Richard Leir-Carleton (died 1933).*

M. McGarvie, 'The Priory, Ditcheat, Somerset', *Trans. Anc. Mons. Soc.*

General Leir-Carleton died in 1933 at the age of ninety-two. His heir, his nephew Hugh Charles Musgrove, had long since settled in Canada but, a true Leir, he could not ignore his inheritance and eventually came to live in the house at Ditcheat then known as the Priory which he renamed Abbey House. Like a true Leir he reached the age of ninety, dying in 1971. But then facts had to be faced; the house was in a poor state and in 1975 it was sold. In the following year, on the death of Robert Beckett Marriott Leir, the advowsons of Ditcheat and Charlton passed from the family. It was a remarkable record.

Luttrell of Dunster and East Quantoxhead

The Luttrells probably originated in Normandy and were living in the East Midlands in the later part of the twelfth century. Geoffrey Luttrell the first (died 1216/17), a loyal supporter of John as both Count of Mortain and king, married one of the two co-heiresses to the Pagnell estates in Yorkshire and Andrew Luttrell (died 1265) successfully claimed land in Lincolnshire and in Somerset from the same family (who gave their name to Newport Pagnell). Andrew served as sheriff of Lincolnshire in 1251 and followed his ancestors as patron of religious houses at Roch, Drax, Nostell and the Gaunts, Bristol. The elder branch of the family, based at Irnham in Lincolnshire, were later to commission the famous Luttrell Psalter.

The younger branch begins with Andrew's younger son Alexander, who left home to settle far away in the Pagnell home at East Quantoxhead where, though not in exactly the same house, the head of the family, Sir Walter Luttrell, still lives. Alexander probably died abroad in or before 1273 serving on a crusade in the retinue of the Lord Edward, later Edward I. His son Andrew was summoned to fight the Scots in 1301 and was

Court House, East Quantoxhead, 1845, by W. W. Wheatley.

SAS

knighted. His son Alexander was knighted at Edward III's coronation, married into the Mandeville family, served as a collector of wool for the king in Somerset, and with others was killed at Watchet in 1354 by several unknown assailants. Of Thomas, his son and successor, little is known, but his grandson John was created a Knight of the Bath at Henry IV's coronation and soon afterwards became a royal servant, paid a salary from the revenues of the county. In 1401, when the king needed people in whom he could trust, Sir John was named sheriff. In 1403 he took up arms for the king when the Percies, the Mortimers and Owen Glendower ganged up together, but before he left he drew up a will dated 20 May appointing his cousin Sir Hugh Luttrell heir to his manor of East Quantoxhead. The seal attached to the will was not his, which was a problem. A supplementary will dated 4 June was proved on 4 August. In between, on 21 July, Henry IV had won the bloody battle of Shrewsbury. Sir John Luttrell was probably among the dead.

Most of his estates passed to a younger branch of the family who held land in Devon, but this younger branch had powerful connections for Andrew Luttrell, grandson of Sir Andrew of East Quantoxhead, had married a lady of breeding. Elizabeth Luttrell was daughter of Hugh Courtenay, Earl of Devon, and Margaret de Bohun, daughter of the Earl of Hereford and Essex; and she was already widow of John de Vere, a son of the Earl of Oxford. Courtenays were to become Archbishop of Canterbury, Lieutenant of Ireland and Governor of Calais. That was power.

She and her new husband went on pilgrimage to Compostella in 1361 with a suitable retinue and were in receipt of a handsome annuity from the Crown. They were evidently personally known to the Black Prince and his wife. Andrew died about 1380. Before that time his wife made a considerable investment: for the sum of over £3333 she bought the reversion of Dunster from Lady Joan Mohun (see below under Mohun). She herself did not survive to enjoy her investment as she died in 1395 and was buried in Exeter. Her heir was her second son Sir Hugh Luttrell.

Sir Hugh was a soldier. He began his military career as an esquire in the household of John of Gaunt and then evidently moved to the service of Richard II. Twice he went with the king to Ireland but passed easily into the service of the new king, Henry IV, like his relatives the Courtenays. By the end of 1399 he was lieutenant to Sir Peter Courtenay as Captain of Calais, and continued in that post under John Beaufort, Earl of Somerset. In 1403 he was an ambassador negotiating with France and Burgundy. In the next year he was Mayor of Bordeaux and was elected MP. He was to hold a Somerset county seat four times and a Devon one once between then and 1415. He had already inherited East Quantoxhead and now, with the death of Lady Mohun, Dunster was his, except that the lady had powerful heirs. Not until 1406 was the matter entirely settled in Sir Hugh's favour.

Household accounts for part of Sir Hugh's time at Dunster have been preserved and tell of many comings and goings, some domestic, some of national significance, for Sir Hugh was Lieutenant of Harfleur, the entry port to Henry V's French empire, for four years from 1417 and Seneschal of Normandy 1419–21. The accounts portray a man of taste, especially a taste for silver plate. Sir Hugh died in 1428, probably on a visit to his daughter in the abbey at Shaftesbury.

Sir Hugh Luttrell was an outstanding man. His son John, who had been very much involved with the building works at Dunster Castle, survived his father by two years and his heir was his second son James, a minor. He took over the estates in 1447 but the Courtenay family had something of a stranglehold on them as his former guardians and in 1450 James was married at the Courtenays' Powderham Castle to Elizabeth Courtenay. It was natural that James should follow the political lead of his father-in-law and thus he fought for the Lancastrians at the battle of Wakefield in 1460 and was knighted by the Duke of Somerset on the battlefield. Seven weeks later he appeared for Queen Margaret at St Albans where he was mortally wounded. The victor and new king, Edward IV, took vengeance on his opponents and the estates of the late Sir James Luttrell were confiscated and later handed over to William Herbert, Baron Herbert and later still Earl of Pembroke.

Incised monument to Lady Elizabeth Luttrell (died 1493), Dunster church.
H. C. Maxwell Lyte,
History of Dunster (1909)

When Henry Tudor won Bosworth field in 1485 the Lancastrians were back and Hugh Luttrell, son of Sir James, soon had Dunster returned to him. He was sheriff in 1488–9, he opposed Perkin Warbeck in 1497 and in 1513 served at sea, having already in his improvements at Minehead's harbour shown his interest in matters maritime. His son Andrew married a daughter of Thomas Wyndham of Felbrigg and also served as sheriff. Both men lived not at Dunster (which the Herberts had seriously neglected) but at East Quantoxhead where both were buried. Andrew, with an eye to insuring his family's future, left a silver cup to Thomas Cromwell. His widow Margaret was well able to look after herself; she went into the shipping business and invested her money in the dissolved Dunster priory.

John Luttrell, her son, went into royal service thanks to Cromwell, was knighted in 1544 by Sir Edward Seymour outside captured Edinburgh, and was in the vanguard at the battle of Pinkie, Seymour's great triumph, in 1547. For three years he served, not always successfully, in Scotland and in the end was taken prisoner, but his triumphal return was rewarded by the government with cash for wages owed. He died, not much over thirty, in 1551 preparing to follow Thomas Wyndham on a madcap venture to Morocco.

Sir John left three daughters; his brother Thomas succeeded as heir to two-thirds of the estate. Thomas was one of the first two MPs elected by the newly-incorporated borough of Minehead, which was to provide a haven for successive members of the Luttrell family and their friends interested in politics. Thomas's heir George sat for the borough twice but like his father quarrelled with the town and tried to have it disenfranchised. He employed the architect William Arnold at Dunster Castle, beginning its transformation to a country house, and substantially rebuilt the house at East Quantoxhead. Much of his energy was spent on conducting lawsuits.

Above: *George Luttrell (died 1629).*
H. C. Maxwell Lyte,
History of Dunster (1909)

Left: *Sir John Luttrell (died 1551).*
H. C. Maxwell Lyte,
History of Dunster (1909)

His second wife, Silvestra, remarried after his death in 1629 and evidently made her new husband's life a misery, for which he heartily forgave her but left her a book on piety, 'desiring that she better love and effect the same than hitherto she hath done'. He left a servant a small sum 'who hath lived under the tyranny of my wife, to the danger of his life, during the space of two years'.

The Luttrells were Parliamentarian in sympathy and Thomas Luttrell held Dunster Castle until 1643 when Francis Wyndham persuaded him to sur-render it. Having been 'fined' £1000 he died in 1644. His son George was acceptable to the government and served as sheriff in 1652–3 but died in 1655 aged only thirty, to be followed by his brother Francis who lasted only until 1666. Francis, second son of Francis, was associated with a curious 'might-have-been': for the sum of £1000 Francis might have been made an earl, the king having given the Bishop of Oxford a patent for one who would contribute that sum to finish the great gate of Christchurch, Oxford.

In the event he remained untitled but served as MP for Minehead. He was a colonel of militia at the time of Monmouth's rebellion, but was an early and strong supporter of William of Orange and founded a regiment which eventually became the Green Jackets. He, too, died at just over thirty in 1690 leaving enormous debts brought about by profligate spending on clothes (but he may surely be forgiven the great staircase at Dunster Castle).

The next Luttrell, Tregonwell, died at twenty to be followed by his soldier uncle Alexander; Alexander's son Alexander died in 1737 aged just thirty-two. His only child by his Trevelyan wife was Margaret, who succeeded to huge debts at the age of eleven. She was brought up at Tetton and married at twenty-one her second cousin Henry Fownes of Nethway in Devon. Under the will of his late father-in-law he took the name Luttrell and promised to live at Dunster Castle for six months every year. Henry proved in every way a satisfactory owner of the estate, creating the park at Dunster (he was fond of horses and hounds) and continuing the work of Dorothy Luttrell, his wife's grandmother, at the castle. Politics and the disposal of his influence at Minehead concerned both Henry (died 1780) and his son John (died 1816); from 1774 until 1790 they were able to name both members, and John generally sold one seat and gave the other to one of his sons. John and his son, also John, continued to control the borough until it was disenfranchised in 1832.

G. F. Luttrell, DL, JP (died 1910).

Mates

Neither the younger John nor his brother Henry married. The next brother, Francis, who had been wounded at Waterloo, died in 1862, so the heir in 1867 to over 15,000 acres of the Dunster estate was his son George. George Fownes Luttrell, in employing the architect Anthony Salvin to transform the seventeenth-century country house on its hilltop site, created a medieval castle to beat all castles – in profile. Within, between 1867 and 1872, his genius created a Victorian home fit for a prosperous country squire; outside (although many visitors fail to see the original Norman motte) they get as good an idea of a medieval stronghold as anywhere.

George Luttrell began opening the castle to the public in the 1870s in aid of the village hospital and proved a model landlord, concerned to improve the lot of his tenants in spite of the agricultural depression which hit his pocket as well as theirs. His son Alexander died in 1944 unprepared for the financial attack far more deadly than an enemy had ever employed against his family. The demands for death duties forced Geoffrey Luttrell to sell most of the 8600-acre Dunster estate in 1949 but he managed to pass the castle and its grounds to his son Walter (now Sir Walter) on his death in 1957. Castle, gardens and park were handed over to the National Trust in 1976.

George Fownes Luttrell had served as sheriff in 1874–5, his grandson Geoffrey in 1935–6 and his great grandson Walter in 1960–1. The last, educated at Eton and Oxford, saw service with the King's Royal Hussars and was awarded the MC in 1945. He was appointed to the lieutenancy in 1960 and was Lord-Lieutenant of Somerset 1978–94. His signal service was marked by his appointment as KCVO in 1993.

Lyte of Lytes Cary

John and Thomas Lyte of Lytes Cary, grandfather and grandson, were justifiably proud of their family. Its origins were modest enough, back in the reign of Henry III when William the Little (le Lyte) was mentioned in deeds which Thomas still possessed and evidently pored over in the early seventeenth century. The same William, perhaps acting only as a loyal neighbour should, found himself on the wrong side of the law in 1265 when that neighbour, Brian de Goviz, was declared a rebel supporter of Simon de Montfort. Based on those deeds Thomas compiled a remarkable pedigree in which he described William as a sergeant at law who proved prosperous enough to add a north aisle to his parish church at Charlton Mackrell, where he and his first wife were buried. The tomb had carved stone figures of the deceased, and in glass the portraits of William in his legal finery and of his second wife. The tomb has long since been removed from the Lyte aisle to the churchyard where it is all but destroyed. The glass has gone completely, but Thomas Lyte's sketch of it was included in his family pedigree.

Sketch of window memorial to William le Lyte and his wife, once in Charlton Mackrell church.

SASP xxxviii

William's successors were not particularly distinguished if the surviving records are any guide. Peter, possibly a grandson, who died in 1348 was probably responsible for building the chapel at Lytes Cary, originally a detached building in front of the house. His son Edmund may be said to be the first family historian because of the accidental burning of his family papers at Draycott early in the reign of Richard II. In 1383, soon after the disaster, he too compiled a family pedigree setting out the various marriages of his ancestors linking the family with minor gentry like themselves but with connections as far away as Devon and Norfolk.

Edmund, evidently a litigious man, served on local juries but never apparently held even minor office, yet when he died in 1418 he held property in neighbouring parishes as well as his own small ancestral estate. Younger sons of such a family had to make their own way; Peter Lyte served under Lord Matravers in a company which mustered at Portsdown for service in France two years after the Agincourt campaign and Philip Lyte was a mounted archer in Sir Hugh Luttrell's company at the same time.

Thomas Lyte, Edmund's grandson, was evidently employed by the canons of Bruton, owners of neighbouring Charlton Adam, and in about 1447 the prior granted him a life pension for his good service. He, or perhaps his son John, built the fine hall which is at the centre of Lytes Cary. John is immortalised because in 1502 his wife was cured of a 'fever quartayn' as a result of prayers to Joseph of Arimathia and the cure was duly recorded in a metrical life of the saint printed in 1520. His wife's name was thought not worth mentioning.

John's son Thomas succeeded in about 1512 and married a Bridgwater lady with money who, after his death, rebuilt part of the family home and then married the head of the Bridgwater customs. One of her younger sons was later to be in charge of all wine coming into the same port, perhaps through the influence of his step-father, more likely because he was in the service of Sir William Capell. Another son, George, was employed by Sir Amias Poulett, governor of Jersey; and yet another, Anthony, served in the royal household under Queen Elizabeth and had a house at Greenwich. He died in 1580. Their eldest brother John was born in 1498. He studied law in London, married a lady named Edith Horsey and in the 1530s began spending money on his house which still bears the date 1533 and his and his wife's coats of arms. Cash evidently ran out and he borrowed £40 from Richard Whiting, the last Abbot of Glastonbury. He repaid the first instalment in May 1537 just after the abbot had finished his dinner in a little room off the great hall of the abbey; the rest was not so forthcoming and the abbot took John to court. With that threat over him he soon repaid the rest in gold, very privately in the abbot's garden, in an arbour of bay, and was given back a small sum on condition he set up the abbot's coat of arms on the new building.

Anthony Lyte (died 1580) and his wife.

SASP xxxviii

The new building does not now, and probably never did, have Whiting's arms, but its windows were once full of heraldic glass recording the families of Horsey and Hussey as well as Lyte. John Lyte was clearly one of the rising gentry of his time; he twice served as escheator of Somerset and Dorset, an office of some considerable profit under the Crown; the rogue from West Somerset, Barnard Dovell, was kept under house arrest at Lytes Cary in 1557. However, most exciting of all was his part in the suppression of the Western Rebellion of 1549 when as a captain of the White Coats, a kind of local militia, he with Sir Hugh Poulett and Sir Thomas Speke captured over a hundred at Kingweston, only a few miles from his home.

Towards the end of his life John Lyte went to live in Sherborne, leaving his house to his heir Henry. Henry was a scholar, probably spent some time in legal training, but is remembered for his work as translator and editor of an authoritative history of plants known as a *Herbal*. The first edition, printed in Antwerp but published in London, appeared in 1578 and was dedicated to Queen Elizabeth. Perhaps overcome by the success of the Herbal he wrote a book called *The Light of Britayne* which proved to his own satisfaction that the British were descended from the Trojans. This he presented to the Queen in 1588 when she went to St Paul's to give thanks for the overthrow of the Armada. Henry then went on to prove that the Lytes sprang from ancient stock which went to Troy and came to Britain with Brutus.

Henry Lyte (died 1607), author of the Herbal.

SASP xxxviii

Henry Lyte died in 1607. His son and successor Thomas, educated at Sherborne, Oxford and the inns of court, was as keen as his father on genealogy and equally keen on royal patronage. Thus after some seven years of labour he produced the royal family line of James I back to Brutus. Both the king and the Prince of Wales were so impressed that they each presented Thomas with a jewel with the donor's portrait in gold surrounded by diamonds. Thomas duly had his own portrait painted with one of the jewels hanging round his neck. Then he proceeded to compile pedigrees of his own family and, sensible genealogist that he was, declared that he did it 'not for any ostentation of birth or kindred … but only that those that are so lately descended of one parentage and from one family might not be strangers one to another'. It was, for its time, an amazing and, so far as one can tell, entirely authentic piece of research, full of such detail as that one was burnt to death as a small boy, another drowned in a well, a third fell from a horse, a fourth drowned at sea. One wife was described candidly as 'not so fortunate as fair'. And one of the pedigrees, the descendants of John and Edith Lyte, all 838 of them, was illustrated.

Thomas has left behind a commonplace book which reveals what a careful researcher he was, for he notes the deeds upon which his work was based and also a large number of other papers including recipes for medicines, cookery notes, notes on farming and gardening, antiquarian material, prayers, biblical quotations, bills, records of family legal disputes and a list of fruit trees growing around his house including 60 different types of apple and 44 kinds of pear.

Thomas Lyte died in 1638 and the genius of the family seems to have died with him. His grandson Henry (by his son also Henry who died in 1666) married a Hippisley and died in 1711. Two sons, including yet another Henry, had died before him, the young Henry in 1685 at the age of twenty-four but described as a captain suggesting a position in the local militia. The heir in 1711 was Henry's youngest brother Thomas Lyte, a successful lawyer, but after his death in 1748 the family seems to have come to financial grief. It must have been a bitter blow for the family to leave the place they had owned for five hunded years, but Thomas Lyte, three generations removed from Thomas the genealogist, sold much of his estate to trustees in return for an annuity and he and his son John finally departed in 1755, settling apparently first at Pilton and then further away in Bath. Henry Maximilian, John's elder son, joined the army, later became a navy agent and was in some way involved in the Stock Exchange fraud of 1814. Thomas, the younger son, was also an army officer whose three children were born in southern Scotland, far away from the ancestral home. The second was the famous clergyman-poet Henry Francis, curate of Brixham and author of the hymn curiously associated with Cup Final football. His grandson Henry Maxwell (the Maxwell from his grandmother whose Irish clergyman father was a friend of Dr Johnson) was perhaps the most remarkable member of the family. For forty years he was Deputy Keeper of the Public Records and had, according to his obituary, 'a strong claim to be regarded as the official founder of the modern school of archivists'. His personal interest was in genealogy, but soon after he left Oxford he wrote a history of his old school, Eton, and not many years later, during which he had scoured many a country house and sorted and listed their archives, he had written a history of his university. His mastery of the archives at

Dunster Castle revealed the Luttrells to themselves and to the world. Sir Henry, as he had come to be known, retired in 1926 and was still working, from his late wife's home at Dinder House, within a few days of his death in 1940 at the age of ninety-two. His editions of many vital Somerset historical records were an amazing contribution from a remarkable man who possessed in full measure the fascination for family history and for records so well demonstrated by several of his ancestors.

Henry Lyte's autograph.

SASP xxxviii

Medlycott of Ven

James Medlycott was a London dyer of Shropshire origins who married the daughter of a Newbury businessman. Their eldest son Thomas was born in the parish of St Botolph, Aldersgate, and attended the Merchant Taylors' school in the city. He spent a year at Christ's College, Cambridge, and passed on to the Middle Temple, where he was called to the bar in 1653 and later became bencher, reader and treasurer.

By 1672 he was well settled in Abingdon and from 1675 was recorder of the borough, the town's chief magistrate. He also sat on the Berkshire bench but was evidently still in practice, for he defended a group of Baptists while declaring himself a 'true son of the Church of England as now established'. His house in East St Helen's was evidently the best in the town and was selected as a lodging for William of Orange on his march to London in 1688.

At a disturbed election in January 1689 Medlycott was chosen as one of the borough's MPs and proved an active politician, much in favour of turning the Convention into a Parliament. But his time there was short for his election was declared void in May. A few months later he was replaced as recorder. Presumably he retained his interests in London but eventually moved to Ven in Milborne Port, which Medlycott's elder son James had bought in 1698 and which gave him a considerable influence in that borough. Thomas died at Ven in 1716.

James himself, also a lawyer and from 1706 a master in chancery (he sold the office for £3000), sat for Milborne Port as a Whig between 1710 and 1722. Probably after he left Parliament he built the great mansion at Ven, which was not quite finished when he died, almost bankrupt, in 1731. His younger brother Thomas, rather more of a politician but with lucrative employment in Ireland, had already sat for Milborne Port between 1705 and 1708 and for Westminster 1708–15. He sat again for Milborne from 1727 until he was ousted by his nephew Thomas, son of James, in 1734. At his death four years later he left most of his estate to an illegitimate son.

The younger Thomas had to resign after an election in 1741 rather than face an expensive petition which he might well have lost, but the government,

Ven House, Milborne Port. Wash drawing by J. Buckler, 1843.

SAS

recognising his value as owner of at least one Parliamentary seat, appointed him while he was out of the Commons a commissioner of hawkers and pedlars and a commissioner of taxes. He returned in 1747 and sat until his death in 1763 but was always in financial difficulties and in receipt of a substantial secret service pension in order to keep control of the borough. His grovelling letters to the Duke of Newcastle show his gratitude but a wish to increase its size. He died childless and was succeeded by his nephew Thomas Hutchings, who, of course, changed his name to Medlycott.

The saga of expensive elections involving varying degrees of bribery and corruption continued at Milborne Port until the two seats were abolished under the Reform Act of 1832, but after an expensive election in 1796 William Coles Medlycott seems to have stood back from intervention, being content to lease some of his property in the borough to the Earl of Uxbridge, thus giving the Tories complete control. The reward for such withdrawal was a baronetcy, conferred on William in 1808.

The 1st baronet died in 1835; his son and namesake altered his home by employing Decimus Burton to replace the ancient farmhouse on one side by offices and to balance it on the other with a large conservatory. The 2nd Sir William, was followed by his four sons in turn, the last of whom, the Revd Sir Hubert James Medlycott, died in 1920. The estate had never been large, like that of Montacute not large enough to support the house. Sir Edward Bradford Medlycott (died 1902) had spent a good deal of time and money on the gardens in the 1890s, but ten years later the family had moved to Sandford Orcas Manor and Ven was occupied by a succession of

tenants. Like many another family in this volume and many more in other parts of England, the Medlycotts sold much of their land between 1918 and 1925. Only in 1957 could they bring themselves to sell Ven and its fine gardens.

The contribution of the Medlycotts to Milborne Port was immense, though the cynic might suggest that their gifts for the public good, like a fire engine in 1733, were not altogether altruistic. After 1832 there was no need to bribe electors but over the next fifty years the name of Sir William Coles Medlycott was associated with building a school, a vicarage house and the double fives court in the centre of the village, and with restoration and extension of the parish church.

Technically, of course, by going to Sandford Orcas they had left Somerset, for the parish with its neighbours had been transferred to Dorset in 1896. Herbert Mervyn, the 7th baronet (1874–1964), was governor of Sherborne's two public schools, chairman of the town's hospital and chairman of the rural district council. His sons, like himself and his father, had been to

Harrow, but while the elder son and eventually the 8th baronet, went on to Cambridge like father and grandfather, Thomas Anthony Hutchings, the younger son, became an architect and left his mark in Milborne Port in the form of the present vicarage house designed in 1937. Mervyn Tregonwell, Anthony's son, succeeded his uncle in 1986 and, as befits someone with such a long pedigree, he is a distinguished genealogist, founder, former honorary secretary and now president of the Somerset and Dorset Family History Society.

Mohun of Dunster

Dunster Castle.

Devon County Council

William de Mohun, lord of Moyon near St Lo in the Cotentin peninsula of Normandy, probably had his home in Somerset chosen for him. William the Conqueror needed trusted lieutenants to secure his kingdom and William was trusted enough to have been given more than fifty manors in Somerset and more in Dorset, Devon and Wiltshire. His particular task was to secure the coastline against possible invasion from supporters of the fallen House of Wessex, and for that reason he turned the natural outcrop of rock above the little River Avill into what Domesday Book called the Castle of Torre. The 'W, sheriff of Somerset' mentioned in 1084 and 1086 was evidently the same William Mohun, and he and his wife were the founders of what became Dunster Priory.

William Mohun the second, probably a younger son of the first William, was influential in national affairs. He enthusiastically took the part of the Empress Matilda in her struggle against King Stephen, for which the king twice came against him in force; and from Matilda in 1141 he received the earldom of Somerset as reward. He may well soon after have withdrawn his support, for the Empress's son Henry, later Henry II, followed Stephen in not recognising the earldom. William certainly used the title when he founded the priory at Bruton in about 1142 and probably survived to see the Empress's son on the throne she had been unable to capture. His son, the third William Mohun, was more modest, enjoying his possessions on both sides of the English Channel until his death in 1176; and his grandson, a fourth William, did the same but, in granting his mill at Minehead to the canons of Bruton, stipulated that the income should provide them with a special meal once a year, to be enjoyed on the day of his death 'if he die on his pilgrimage from Jerusalem'. A sort of return ticket. He died in 1193, but whether at home or abroad is not known.

Reginald Mohun, the next owner of Dunster, had some trouble with King John, who evidently acquired some of his Normandy lands by force, but he remained loyal in spite of all, taking a ship to France in 1206 and going with John to Ireland in 1210. He died, still young, in 1213 and the lands of the heir, another Reginald, were divided between the king and his supporters, among whom was the powerful William Brewer, the young boy's grandfather. The young man was knighted in 1227 and served the king in France and Wales. In the 1230s he became a royal judge and some years later keeper of royal forests.

Reginald Mohun the second improved his castle at Dunster by building the lower ward in stone, and he is remembered as a generous benefactor not only to the family's 'favourite' monasteries at Dunster and Bruton but also to Barlinch Priory and Cleeve Abbey. His most generous benefaction, however, was to be the foundation of the Cistercian Abbey of Newenham in Devon in 1246. A story, probably later invented by the monks of Newenham, told how Reginald had actually visited Pope Innocent IV at Lyons and had been rewarded by him with the title of Earl of Est, interpreted as Somerset. Just possibly the pope had made him a Count Palatine as well as presenting him with a golden rose, which was also part of the story. Certainly he had been present at Newenham in 1254 and had laid three foundation stones for the buildings then rising. He died early in January 1258 at his grandfather's house at Torre and was buried as a founder deserved at Newenham.

The pious Reginald was followed by his grandson John, who duly served Edward I in Wales against Prince Llewellyn but died two years later so that the Dunster estates were again in Crown hands. When his heir, another John, eventually succeeded he took up a military career, serving in Gascony, Flanders, Wales and Scotland. His extensive lands made him a natural candidate for summons to the emerging Parliament, and he was called on every occasion it met between 1299 and 1330, although in 1329 he had permission to send a younger son Robert in his place. His eldest son would have been the normal substitute, but the next John Mohun, who also fought in Scotland, had died. In 1330 another grandson succeeded as a child to the Dunster estate, and another John. He, too, was a soldier, fighting as usual in Scotland and in France; he was present at Crecy and fought under the Black Prince and John of Gaunt. Like his grandfather he was regarded as a notable feudal baron, although without formal title, and was summoned to Parliament between 1342 and 1374.

Sir John Mohun died without a male heir in 1375. Longstanding debts had forced him into a series of complicated legal arrangements whereby Dunster, Minehead and Kilton had been promised to Lady Elizabeth Luttrell. In 1376 the sale was completed in the sum of 5000 marks (£3333.33p) but there was one condition: Lady Joan Mohun should remain in possession for her lifetime. The Luttrells had to wait for thirty years before Dunster was surely theirs, for when Joan died in 1404 there were three claimants prepared to challenge the former agreement. The claimants were formidable because they were landed and titled, for Elizabeth Mohun had married William Montacute, Earl of Salisbury, one of the original Knights of the Garter, Philippa Mohun had married as her third husband Edward, Duke of York, and Maud had married Sir John Strange of Knockin. The Countess of Salisbury, the Duke of York (killed at

Agincourt) and Maud's son Richard gave Sir Hugh Luttrell some anxious moments and cost him money, but Dunster proved securely his. Some other parts of the Mohun estate certainly passed to Lord Strange of Knockin, and there were those who claimed that the barony of Dunster passed to the Stanleys, Earls of Derby.

Opposite, Left: *Effigy of Joan, Lady Mohun (died 1404), in Canterbury Cathedral; engraved C. A. Stothard, 1817.*

C. A. Stothard, *Monumental Effigies of Great Britain* (1817)

Right: *Effigy of Philippa, Duchess of York (died 1431) in Westminster Abbey; engraved by C. A. Stothard (1817).*

C. A. Stothard, *Monumental Effigies of Great Britain* (1817)

$$\diamond\diamond\blacklozenge\diamond\diamond$$

Phelips of Montacute

The Phelipses probably came from Wales, perhaps from Carmarthen, from which another branch settled in Pembrokeshire in the late-fifteenth century. That was the time when a David Phelips (as it will be simpler to spell the West Country branch) set up a business in Bristol; his brother Thomas was living at Lufton, not far from Montacute, by 1460. The effigy of David Phelips in the family aisle at Montacute parish church perhaps represents their father, another David, who may, of course, have never left Wales but who was revered by later generations as the founder of their dynasty (and naturally, as a gentleman, was portrayed in armour).

The name David is a second clue to their Welsh origins, but Thomas was the more popular, both within the family and outside, to the confusion of historians. There were certainly far too many Thomases in the mid sixteenth century for comfort. What characterised the first of his name was business acumen, something he shared with his two sons and a grandson. By 1460 he was in the service of the Brook family, who owned land in Somerset, Devon and Kent, and in their service he rose from yeoman in 1460 to gentleman in 1466 to esquire in 1482. On the way he served as escheator of Somerset and Dorset in 1471 and 1478, became collector of customs at Bridgwater in 1471 and probably very soon afterwards moved to Montacute where he began leasing houses from Montacute Priory in the centre of the village. In the early 1480s he also had shares in some Bridgwater ships and when he died in 1500 he was prominent enough to request burial before the high altar of Montacute's priory church, surely a position reserved for patrons and the most generous donors. The only copy of his will is in the cathedral library at Canterbury, for at the time of his death there was no Archbishop of Canterbury and the prior of Christchurch thus took over his lucrative probate work.

Thomas had two sons, Thomas and Richard. Thomas was overshadowed by his brother. He came to live in Montacute from Dorset long after their father's death in one of the houses leased from the priory, and after its dissolution he took on more of the former monastic land. Before then, from 1536 onwards, he made himself useful to the rising man of the day, Edward Seymour, who took full advantage of the fact that his sister Jane was

Queen. One of Seymour's many acquisitions was Muchelney Abbey, and Thomas leased some of its rich pastures as well as sending timber from some of the demolished buildings to his patron.

Thomas Phelips died in 1565 and was succeeded there by his nephew, another Thomas, eldest son of his brother Richard. Richard himself was probably a lawyer whose ability in land management brought him employment with the Grey family, Marquesses of Dorset, owners of Sock Dennis near Ilchester, with Edward Seymour and later with Henry Courtenay, Marquess of Exeter. Even before that he may have had a junior post in the royal household, thanks to the influence of Giles, Lord Daubeney, owner of nearby Barrington. Such connections brought him lucrative posts such as butler of Lyme Regis and Weymouth, collector of customs at Poole, under-sheriff of Somerset and Dorset. He served in parliament five times, twice for Poole, once for Melcombe Regis, once for either Wareham or Weymouth, and once for Dorset (when his own son Thomas was MP for Melcombe Regis). His country home was at Charborough in Dorset.

Richard died in 1558 leaving the one son he trusted, Thomas, as his sole executor. One other son, William, his wife and their daughter were given modest allowances under his will. There was a proper silence about his son Henry who, after spending twenty years as a student, robbed his parents and fled to the continent where, as a convinced Catholic, he betrayed the Protestant William Tyndale to the government of Charles V.

Thomas the son may well have been a lawyer and was fond of quoting Latin tags in his letters. While his father lived he was somebody, representing Wareham, Melcombe Regis and Poole a total of six times in parliament, but after his death he seems to have retired – one historian says he did not cut much of a figure for the remaining thirty years of his life. He was, of course, still somebody in Montacute and owner of lands in surrounding parishes; and by his wife, a daughter of the merchant Matthew

Monuments to Thomas Phelips (died 1588) and his wife, Montacute church.
SASP lxxiv

Smyth of Bristol, he had four sons and four daughters. John, the eldest son, settled in Dorset at Corfe Mullen; Richard and yet another Thomas were in other ways not satisfactory. So he left to son Edward his house in Montacute with the instruction that Edward was to pay his eldest brother £650 for it.

Edward was undoubtedly the greatest member of his family: MP six times including twice for Somerset, and Speaker of the House of Commons between 1604 and 1611; a lawyer with a large London practice appointed a King's Sergeant in 1603 and a senior judge (Master of the Rolls) in 1611. He took part in several famous trials including those of Sir Walter Raleigh and the Gunpowder Plotters. He is remembered best of all in Somerset for building Montacute House, one of the great country houses of its period in England, designed by William Arnold, a local mason/architect, probably a native of Charlton Musgrove. The dates 1598, 1599 and 1601 are found in parts of the house.

Montacute House, the Great Chamber, 1844; lithograph by W. L. Walton of a drawing by J. Harding from a sketch by C. J. Richardson.

SAS

As Speaker, Sir Edward (knighted in 1603) earned the reputation for being too closely associated with the Crown. His son and heir, Robert, a politician pure and simple, could never have been accused of such compliance. He was knighted with his father in 1603 and sat in every parliament but one (when he was appointed sheriff to stop him from standing) between 1604 and 1629; but from the early 1620s he was normally leading the opposition to the king. He spent eight months in the Tower in 1621–2, objected to forced loans and other kinds of doubtfully legal taxation and in his last parliament began the kind of opposition to Charles I which was to lead to

Civil War. A fellow MP described him as a 'little dark man' whose speeches were 'ready and spirited'. One of his particular political enemies was his near neighbour John, Baron Poulett of Hinton St George. One of his greatest weaknesses was his abominable handwriting.

Sir Robert died in 1638. His eldest son Edward, usually known as Colonel after the rank he held in the royal army during the Civil War, was disqualified from sitting as an MP after war broke out, but sat in Charles I's parliament at Oxford, surrendered at Exeter in 1646 and in 1650 was living under house arrest at Wells. He and his brother Robert, another royalist colonel, took a great risk in being involved in the escape of Charles II to France in 1652.

Sir Robert Phelips (died 1638).
National Portrait Gallery

At the Restoration Colonel Sir Edward became part of the Establishment, was MP for Somerset between 1661 and 1678 and generally lived the life of a country gentleman ready to support the king's government by serving as a magistrate and a deputy lieutenant. He died in 1679. Robert was more committed to the king's cause. He served as Groom of the Bedchamber to the king from 1661 until Charles's death and under James II was a commissioner for the great wardrobe and for the privy seal, and in 1687–9 was Chancellor of the Duchy of Lancaster. Probably through the influence of his cousins he was returned for Stockbridge to the Cavalier Parliament and he sat for Andover in 1685. Lord Shaftesbury marked him down as 'vile' and accused him of accepting huge bribes; he certainly held some valuable Crown leases but had to mortgage and then to sell his wife's estate at Redlynch to Stephen Fox to make ends meet. After James II's fall he was a non-juror, and his epitaph in Bath Abbey asserted that he 'stood out as a steadfast and energetic champion of the English church and the lawful monarchy… The times changed, but he did not change with them'.

Robert's nephew Edward was of the same mould; MP for the family borough of Ilchester in the Cavalier Parliament, returned there again in 1685 and for the county in 1690 and 1698. He was active in the county's horse militia for much of his life though he was considerably embarrassed in 1685 when his men would not serve him against the Duke of Monmouth. That was partly because he had made himself personally unpopular with his antagonism towards recusants and dissenters; he was said to have been 'very successful in bring non-conformists to Church' and acted with aggression against radicals in Taunton and Bridgwater. Even the king thought his arbitrary searches of suspects unnecessary. He was later summoned before the Privy Council for his actions in fining the sheriff and was relieved of his office as a magistrate. He declared for the Prince of Orange but in 1696 he was removed from all his offices including his colonelcy of militia horse, the magistracy and his duties as vice-admiral. He died in 1699 leaving three daughters, a serious encumbrance on the estate since they all had to be provided for.

The way round this problem was for the heir, yet another Edward, nephew of the last, to marry one of them. In the event he married two, while the third married into the Mildmay family. Edith Phelips, who was both his aunt and his mother-in-law, retained her share of the estate as well as her own inheritance from her father John Blake, a Langport businessman, until her death in 1728. Edward Phelips attended Oxford University and Lincoln's Inn and represented first the family borough of Ilchester in Queen Anne's reign and from 1722 to 1727 the county and held the office of Comptroller of the Mint 1711–14. He was a Tory and in 1721 he was named as a probable supporter should the Old Pretender choose to invade. He died in 1734 and was followed by his son by his second wife, another Edward, who attended Westminster School before Oxford and who sat for Somerset 1774–80. He did not distinguish himself as a parliamentarian; he was said to have been 'much fitter for parish or turnpike business', and he certainly never served as sheriff. But, thanks to inheriting property from a nephew and an aunt, he was able to improve the estate and, with a clear conscience, indulge in his great love of hunting. His improvements to Montacute House included the addition of the Clifton Maybank west front which provided better access between the two ends of the building.

Edward Phelips, the eldest son of the last, sat for the county 1784–92, having followed his father from Westminster to Oxford but then having gone on to the Middle Temple. He was a staunch supporter of Pitt. His career was, however, short; he died within his father's lifetime and the estate passed to his next brother William, then vicar of Yeovil, the first of several members of the family to take Holy Orders. William's son John was chairman of the Somerset Quarter Sessions and a kindly landlord. At his death in 1834 the heir was his nephew William, then aged only eleven. Improvements were evidently made at Montacute from the 1840s onwards, but William's ill health probably brought them to a halt and brought the estate almost to insolvency. A house on such a grand scale needed a large estate to maintain it. William Robert Phelips (1846–1919) had to preside over the sale of plate and pictures and then of the farms which constituted what remained of the estate.

William Robert's sons Edward Frederick (died 1928) and Gerald Almarus (died 1940) both found the house impossible. It was actually valued at under £6000 'for scrap' when in 1931 it was acquired by the Society for the Protection of Ancient Buildings and passed to the National Trust. 75,593 people visited it in 2000–1. The family, of course, continued; no longer country gentlemen, but David Phelips, the head of the line, was in the sugar business and a cousin was a senior local-government officer who, in retirement, became fascinated with the history of the family and contributed much to the knowledge of its early history.

John Phelips (died 1834).
C. Lines, *Montacute and the Phelips Family*

Opposite: *Montacute House, built by Sir Edward Phelips c. 1600.*

SAS

Portman of Orchard

Edward Berkeley Portman of Orchard Portman, Somerset and of Bryanston, Dorset, Baron and Viscount Portman, Lord-Lieutenant of Somerset 1839–64, bore two distinguished Somerset names. Such were the complications of landed families, however, that both Henry Seymour in 1690 and William Berkeley in about 1736 were both obliged to change their surnames in order to succeed to the family estates.

The 'pure' Portmans, men of the market, were Taunton merchants at least as far back as the reign of Edward I. The family later believed that Thomas Portman's grandfather bore a coat of arms, which is less than likely; Thomas himself sat for the borough in parliament in 1302 and 1312. Two generations later William Portman, son of Richard, was elected for the borough at least eleven times between 1362 and 1406. His willingness to pay his own expenses rather than popularity or aptitude for politics may be the explanation. He had premises in Fore Street and Cornhill, leased pasture outside the town from the Bishop of Winchester, and arranged a gift of land to the priory in his native town to ensure the right of burial within its walls.

Walter Portman, William's son, succeeded about 1413 and was MP for the borough ten times between 1417 and 1435 and before his death in about 1454 was described as both gentleman and esquire, for as an able lawyer he was retained by the Luttrells, the Hungerfords, the Hills, Simon Raleigh and others and was evidently well known in the courts in London. He had also acquired a landed estate through his marriage to Christine, heiress of William Orchard of Orchard.

John, Walter's son and heir, died in 1521 leaving modest sums of cash to his daughter and two sons; Leonard was to have £10 'to fynde him to scoole if he will be a preest'. Naturally Leonard agreed, went to Oxford, and held livings in Wiltshire and Somerset. The eldest son William, who had to see that his father was buried as he wished before the high cross near the pulpit in Taunton priory church, was given nothing specifically, for he was already launched on a career, admitted to the Middle Temple four years earlier.

William Portman walked with the mighty; his fellow MP for Taunton in 1529 was Thomas Cromwell and among his clients was Bishop Gardiner of Winchester (and possibly even Wolsey). He may have sat twice more but from 1540 until his death in 1557 he dealt with petitions addressed to the House of Lords. As a leading lawyer he took part in the trials of the Duke of Somerset in 1551 and of Sir Nicholas Throckmorton in 1554, was a judge from 1546 and Chief Justice of the King's Bench from 1555. But he was still a landed gentleman, knighted at the coronation of Edward VI, and with some of his fees he and his son Sir Henry bought more estates, not just in and around Taunton but in Devon, Dorset, Hampshire and St Marylebone, Middlesex, the last of which was to make the family's fortune.

Sir Henry's eldest son Hugh was a lawyer and knight of the shire for Somerset in 1597. His vast estate passed to his younger brother John, created a baronet in 1612. The title did not last long, in fact not quite eighty years, for his first son died without children, his second and third died unmarried. His youngest, William, MP for Taunton in the first years of the Long Parliament, was father of Sir William, the last baronet, made Knight of the Bath at Charles II's restoration.

Sir William was a politician at a dangerous time. His father had lost £30,000 during the Civil War, had been fined £7000, and had died a prisoner in the Tower after his capture at Naseby in 1645. But recovery was complete, thanks to three fortunate marriages, and he was able to buy the great estate at Bryanston in East Dorset. In the House of Commons he sat on many committees and in the political crises in the 1680s he was for King and Church and against the succession of the papist Duke of York.

In the summer of 1680 he entertained the Duke of Monmouth at Orchard Portman, but gradually changed his mind and led the East Dorset militia at the battle of Sedgemoor. And, having been one of the first to join William of Orange in 1688, he voted in the Convention that the throne was not vacant. Taunton elected him as its MP for the fifth time in 1690 but he died within ten days. Sir William, educated at Oxford and one of the early members of the Royal Society, was a great local figure; deputy lieutenant and magistrate in Somerset and Dorset and recorder of Taunton. He was remembered for his charity: 'so noble a spirit that the absolute poor do not use to want what he has'. But he had no children and the Portmans were faced with the first of two succession crises caused by the failure of male heirs.

Sir William was succeeded by his cousin Henry Seymour, who changed his name promptly to Portman. Not much else changed; he had already been elected to parliament six times and continued to sit for Taunton, Wells or Somerset in ten more parliaments. Under William III he was thought to be a Jacobite; under Queen Anne he was a Tory and was rewarded with the office of ranger or keeper of Hyde Park. He lost his seat at Taunton in 1715 and died in 1728 aged ninety-three.

Now enter the Berkeleys, for old Henry Seymour/Portman had no children and his heir at his death in 1728 was his distant cousin William Berkeley of

Pylle, a great-great grandson of Sir John Portman, the 1st baronet. Under an Act of Parliament William assumed the additional name of Portman. Eighteenth-century Portmans, enjoying an income of some £8000 a year, usually did their duty in parliament either for Somerset, Wells or Taunton, but after the remodelling of Bryanston by James Wyatt in 1778 the family tended to be more interested in Dorset, for which Edward Berkeley Portman sat as MP between 1806 and 1823. He had succeeded his brother in 1803 when the estate was worth £12,000 a year, but when he won the Dorset seat he was seen as the champion of the yeomanry against the grandees, and he often voted against the government of the day. He died in Rome in 1823.

His son, also Edward, succeeded to his father's Dorset seat in parliament and held it until 1832 when he was elected for St Marylebone, one of the new seats created under the Reform Act. He was known as a moderate Liberal. His marriage to a daughter of the Earl of Harewood, however, brought him into Court circles for she served Queen Victoria as Lady of the Bedchamber from the Queen's accession. He himself had been created Baron Portman of Orchard Portman earlier in 1837, became a councillor for both the Duchy of Cornwall and the Duchy of Lancaster, and between 1865 and 1888 was Lord Warden of the Stanneries. In 1873 he was created Viscount Portman of Bryanston. He was Lord-Lieutenant of Somerset 1839–64.

The first Viscount Portman died at his Dorset home in 1888 in his ninetieth year. In 1876 his estate had amounted to nearly 32 000 acres some, such as Durston and Hestercombe, recently purchased, and it was increased by nearly 2000 acres in the following four years, producing a gross annual income of £100,000. That total did not include the lucrative London property including, of course, Portman and Bryanston Squares. On Lady Day 1888, ninety-nine-year leases on perhaps more than 1750 Marylebone houses fell in, and payments for new leases are said to have produced eight times the normal year's income.

The 2nd viscount had been a Liberal MP for Shaftesbury and for Dorset, but from 1886 was a Liberal Unionist and in 1909 he left the Liberal party because of the socialistic character of the budget. He died in 1919 at the age of ninety leaving property worth over £648,000 net. His son and heir, Edward William Berkeley Portman, of Hestercombe, had already predeceased him in 1911.

After the 2nd viscount's death the destruction of the Portman estate began. Death duties were payable not only on his death but on those of his sons the 3rd and 4th viscounts in 1923 and 1929, forcing the sale of land in both Somerset and Dorset. The family home at Bryanston, rebuilt for the 2nd viscount in the 1890s, was given up for use as a public school in 1927. Worse was to come in the 1940s with the deaths of the 4th viscount's son without male heirs in 1942 and of his uncles the 6th and 7th viscounts in 1946 and 1948. Gerald William Berkeley Portman, son of the last and 8th Viscount Portman, died without children in 1967 and was succeeded by his nephew Edward Henry.

The Rt Hon William Henry Berkeley Portman, DL, JP, 2nd Viscount Portman (died 1919).

Mates

Several of those quickly-passing viscounts shared a love of foxhunting and served their country in the armed forces; two were directors of an insurance company, but they seem not to have been interested in either national politics or local government. By 1976 the family estate had been reduced to 1000 acres and the former land in Somerset had passed to the Crown Estate. The 9th Viscount Portman has a home in Portman Square Mews where earlier Portman tenants had stabled their horses and lodged their grooms, and his family has left Somerset for good.

Former Portman estate farmhouses and cottages in, for instance, Durston, Staple Fitzpaine or Thurlbear bear physical witness to the massive modernising which was undertaken on the estate at the end of the nineteenth century (though one cottage in Durston remains without the typical slate roof and carved bargeboards because the tenant had upset his lordship). Hestercombe House, bought with its estate by the 1st viscount in 1872 for £55,000, was extensively remodelled and partially rebuilt over the next five years or so (one architect was dismissed, replaced and re-engaged), the result being what Nikolaus Pevsner described as in a 'debased "free Renaissance"' style. Beneath its southern terrace, commissioned in 1905 by Edward William Berkeley Portman, the 1st viscount's grandson, lies a fine garden designed by Sir Edwin Lutyens and today planted in the way first planned by Gertrude Jekyll.

Taunton has a Portman ward in its hospital and a Portman Street, and one of its oldest houses was without a doubt one of the many properties which belonged to the family from the fifteenth century until early in the nineteenth. Orchard Portman, proving unhealthy to live in, was pulled down in 1843.

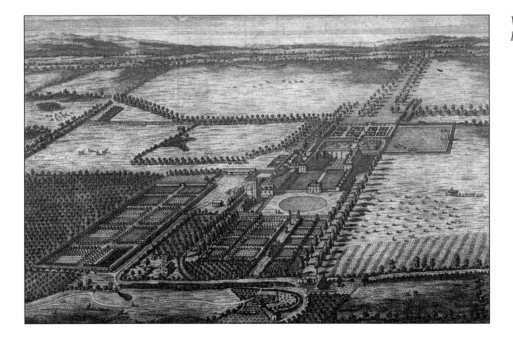

View of Orchard Portman c. 1708; L. Knyff and J. Kip.

L. Knyff and J. Kip,
Britannia Illustrata (1707)

Poulett of Hinton St George

I f ever a family had clear Somerset origins it was the Paulets or Pouletts, although the titles taken by one of its branches, Marquesses of Winchester and Dukes of Bolton, suggest they may just have forgotten. Walter of Pawlett, and who knows how many ancestors, took his name from his native parish on the eastern bank of the River Parrett below Bridgwater. Walter was followed by his son William in 1242–3. By the 1320s the place of origin had become a regular surname and was often spelt Paulet. John Paulet, who died about 1382, married Joan Reigny who brought with her two estates in North Petherton, Melcombe (later Melcombe Paulet) and Rhode. John's eldest son was knighted; his younger son William acquired Beere Manor near Cannington, still not far from the Parrett.

William, Sir John's third son, inherited Melcombe and was the great-great grandfather of that remarkable and pliant civil servant William Paulet, created in 1539 Baron St John of Basing, the great house in Hampshire where he lived, Earl of Wiltshire in 1550 and Marquess of Winchester in 1551. His son John was obliged to sell Melcombe and other Somerset estates including Nunney to pay his father's debts to the Crown at his death in 1572. Charles Paulet, 6th Marquess of Winchester, was created Duke of Bolton in 1689, a title that branch of the family (who now became Powletts) bore until the death without a son of Harry Powlett in 1794. George Paulet, third cousin once removed, became Marquess of Winchester, a title which still survives.

Back in Somerset, Thomas Paulet of Rhode, second son of Sir John, was ancestor of a family who came to be Pouletts and were, as they contributed to national and local affairs, at first regularly knighted, then barons, and finally earls. Thomas's son William, in about 1430, married the heiress Elizabeth Denebaud and acquired with her lands in the south of the county centred on Hinton St George and including Chaffcombe and Shepton Beauchamp. The family was on its way.

For a century and more they played an active part on the national scene. Sir Amias, son of William, probably rebuilt the old Denebaud house at

Hinton, creating what was clearly a significant base for a prominent family. He was a lawyer who opposed Richard III, supported Henry Tudor and was knighted after the battle of Stoke in 1487. He led troops in northern France in 1513 and in the 1520s was much in London. A story that he was under house arrest in the Middle Temple for several years by order of Cardinal Wolsey is unlikely; he acted as a tax collector in Somerset at the time and was also present on that occasion in London when Richard Whiting's election as Abbot of Glastonbury was confirmed. He was then said to be sixty-eight years old; he was thus over eighty when he died at Chaffcombe in 1538.

As men of influence Sir Amias and his son Hugh were both retained by Somerset monasteries; Hugh was surveyor or steward of at least three including Glastonbury. Hugh was also a soldier, serving with distinction in France in 1544, and in 1549 active against the Cornish rebels. In 1559 he became military and civil governor of Jersey, the first of three members of his family to serve there. His eldest son, another Amias, was a friend of Queen Elizabeth's minister Sir Francis Walsingham and in 1576 was employed as ambassador at the French court. For three years from 1585 he had the difficult task of guarding Mary Queen of Scots and was ordered to treat her with severity. Instead, while declaring he would kill her rather than let her escape, he paid the expenses of her large household from his own pocket. He was, with Walsingham, among the commissioners who tried the queen but refused to have her murdered quietly, urging instead that she be executed quickly.

Below left: *Monument to Sir Amias Poulett (died 1538), Hinton St George church.*

SASP lxxii

Below right: *Monument to Sir Hugh Poulett (died 1573), Hinton St George church.*

SASP lxxii

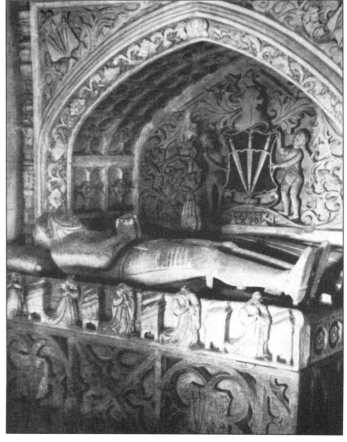

Monument to Sir Amias Poulett (died 1588), Hinton St George church.

SASP lxxiv

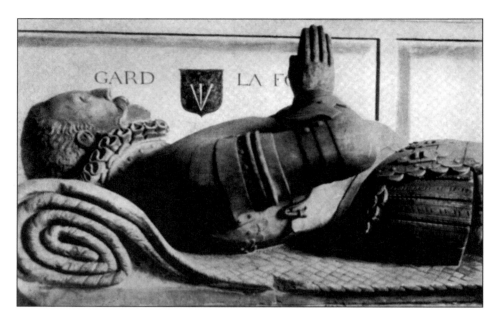

John Poulett, grandson of the diplomat, was an ardent supporter of the Crown. By the time he entertained the young Charles I at Hinton in 1625 he had served three times as MP and had his own cavalry regiment. Much to the annoyance of his neighbour Sir Robert Phelips he was created in 1627 Baron Poulett of Hinton St George. He was evidently a man of action, complaining when he was sheriff in 1616–17 that he was tied to his home – 'this dull, dirty place'; and in 1635 writing to Secretary Conway that the hunting season was over but that, should he come down to Hinton at Christmas, he would show him some 'tricksey lasses'.

Lord Poulett had command of a ship in the Channel Fleet in 1635 but apparently saw no action. That came with the political crisis of 1640 when he was commissioned to treat with the Scots at York on the king's behalf. At the outbreak of war in 1642 he was at Wells and retreated to Sherborne and then to Hinton, where the house was held by about fifty men who told the approaching enemy to 'begone otherwise they would let bullets fly amongst them'. Parliament ordered Poulett's arrest and he was taken at Bridgnorth but escaped and in the next year was serving under Sir Ralph Hopton, the royalist commander in the West, and raising men in Dorset. Later he saw action in Devon and Dorset, beating Sir William Waller at Hemyock, and damaging Lyme when beseiging it. He was arrested when Exeter fell in 1646 and died in 1649, having to pay a fine of £2742, £1500 to Lady Drake in compensation for damage to her house at Ashe, and £200 a year to Lyme.

His son, also John, was no less enthusiastic for the cause of the Crown but his fine for his loyal service in the North, in Ireland, at Winchester against Cromwell, and finally in Exeter was eventually reduced to £3760 thanks to the intervention of Sir Thomas Fairfax, his first wife's brother-in-law. At the end of the war Lord Poulett returned to Hinton where he spent a good deal of money building his bowling green, becoming known for his 'generosity in plentiful housekeeping' and for his 'very beautiful hounds and horses'.

John, the 3rd Baron Poulett, had only just come of age when his father died in 1665 and he himself died before he was forty leaving an estate worth not far short of £5000 a year. The lands of his ancestors had been extended by his grandfather's marriage to Elizabeth Kenn, heiress to an estate in North Somerset including Court de Wick. His own second marriage to a daughter of the Earl of Pembroke showed how far the Pouletts had risen.

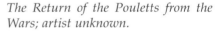

The Return of the Pouletts from the Wars; artist unknown.

C. G. Winn, *The Pouletts of Hinton St George* (1995)

Walton Castle, a folly built by John Poulett, 1st Baron Poulett, 1615-20; S. H. Grimm, 1788.

SAS

And they were to rise further, though yet another John, the 4th baron, began life 'very weak' and 'marvellous infirm' but before he was thirty was said to be 'certainly one of the hopefullest gentlemen in England' though his physical attributes were undistinguished. He was only about ten when his father died and was not involved in politics when the Duke of Monmouth came by his park. William of Orange hunted there in 1688, but he was still not involved and only took his seat in the House of Lords in 1696.

A local story declares that the south front of Hinton House was built to the designs of Inigo Jones to accommodate Queen Anne. The accession of Princess Anne to the throne certainly brought Poulett to prominence, locally as Lord-Lieutenant of Devon and nationally as a Privy Councillor. In 1706 he took part in the discussions which brought about the union of England and Scotland and as reward was created Viscount Hinton St George (a title thereafter used by sons and heirs) and Earl Poulett. For a short time he was one of the Commissioners of the Treasury – presumably because he was a supporter of the Tory politician Robert Harley, from 1711 he was Lord Steward of the Queen's Household, and in 1712 was created a Knight of the Garter. But all was lost for him, Harley and many others when Queen Anne died.

John Poulett, 1st Earl Poulett (died 1743); attributed to Gilson.
C. G. Winn, *The Pouletts of Hinton St George* (1995)

Successive earls thereafter did little that was distinguished, although they dutifully served as Lord-Lieutenant in either Devon or Somerset, commanded the militia in various eighteenth-century crises, and held office as recorders of Bridgwater in order to control the parliamentary elections for the borough. John, the 4th earl, was made a Knight of the Thistle in 1794 and was a Tory Lord of the Bedchamber from 1795 to 1819.

With the 5th earl, one of the few peers who opposed the Reform Bill to the last, family problems began. His three sons by his wife Charlotte, daughter of Henry Berkeley Portman, all died before him unmarried. The title passed to his nephew William Henry, son of Vice-Admiral the Honourable George Poulett. He was a soldier, educated at Sandhurst, who served in two regiments of Foot and was in Afghanistan in 1854. He had three wives, the first the daughter of a Portsmouth pilot who, it later transpired, was already pregnant by him. His son by his third wife, the daughter of an artist, was still under age when he died in 1899.

John Poulett, KT, 4th Earl Poulett (died 1819); after James Northcote.
C. G. Winn, *The Pouletts of Hinton St George* (1995)

William John Lydston Poulett had to take steps to establish his right to the title in 1903 because a rival calling himself Viscount Hinton also claimed the title. That rival was the eldest son of the 6th earl. In July 1905 the Committee of Privileges of the House of Lords rejected the rival's claim on the ground of bastardy although he had been born in wedlock. The unfortunate man died in the Holborn Union Infirmary but his son was left £5000 by the Dowager Duchess of Cleveland and became a tea planter in Ceylon.

The 7th earl, educated at Cambridge, married a chorus girl from the Gaiety Theatre. He served for three years in the Royal Artillery and later in the Anti-Aircraft Corps, but died in the great influenza epidemic in 1918. George Amias Fitzwarrine Poulett, born in 1909, proved to be the 8th and last Earl Poulett. Perhaps the happiest part of his life was when he served at the railway works at Swindon as an apprentice mechanical engineer and later at Reading at the signal factory. He rejoiced in his membership of the

Institute of Railway Signalling Engineers. He died without children in 1973 in Jersey. By that date the family estate, over 22,000 acres almost all in Somerset, had been reduced to lordships of manors; land had been sold in 1912–13, 1941, 1958 and finally 1968 when Hinton House and park went under the hammer and the earl left for the Channel Islands. A memorial to the last earl was placed in the family pew in Hinton St George parish church not far from those of many of his ancestors.

THE CLAIMANTS TO THE POULETT PEERAGE: CLOWN AND FAIRY QUEEN IN THE PAST, THEIR PRESENT, AND THEIR HOPED-FOR FUTURE.   1899

The Poulett peerage claim, 1899.

SAS

Seymour, Dukes of Somerset

The Seymours were an ancient Monmouthshire family traceable back there to the reign of Edward I. Their Somerset connection began with the marriage of Sir Roger Seymour to a Somerset heiress, Cecily Beauchamp, elder sister and co-heir of John, Baron Beauchamp of Hatch. Among their share of the Beauchamp manors in the county were Hatch and Shepton Beauchamp. As a family the Seymours displayed a taste for membership of the House of Commons; William, Roger's son, may have been a retainer of John of Gaunt and sat for Herefordshire in the Cambridge Parliament of 1388. His son, another Roger, married Maud Sturmy, heiress of the Wiltshire manor of Wolfhall in Burbage, where the Tudor part of the house still survives, and that became their principal home for a time, though Roger and Maud were licensed in 1408 to hear Mass in the chapel of their house at Shepton Beauchamp. Their son Sir John (died 1464) sat in parliament once for the Wiltshire borough of Ludgershall and three times for that county, but when he served as sheriff of Somerset and Dorset in 1433–4 (he was sheriff of three other counties and served in all seven times) he was described as of Hatch Beauchamp.

Sir John, who had been constable of Farnham Castle for the Bishop of Winchester and of Marlborough Castle for the Crown did not apparently take sides in the dispute between Lancaster and York, but on several occasions found it necessary to acquire a pardon, for as a public servant in an ever-changing government scene he was bound to have offended one side or the other. He could probably claim to have engineered the return of both of his sons to parliament; John sat four times, Richard twice.

Sir John was followed by his grandson John (died 1491) and he by his son, yet another John. That last Seymour cut a figure at Court where he was already prominent enough to attend the funeral of Henry VII in 1509 and was a knight of the body and a groom of the chamber to the new king. He was present when the king met his two fellow monarchs Francis I of France and the Holy Roman Emperor Charles V, and he was later to entertain Henry VIII at two of his homes. As a man of action he is said to have been knighted for his 'gallant and conspicuous conduct' at the battle of

Blackheath in 1497 when the Cornish rebels supporting Perkin Warbeck were defeated and he was made a knight banneret in 1513 after the battle of the Spurs. In 1522 he was a member of the Duke of Suffolk's army which invaded France.

Sir John's importance does not lie in any of these activities, nor yet as an MP in 1529 and probably in 1536. It lies instead in three of his four children: Edward, the eldest, is better known as Protector Somerset; Thomas, the next, was made Lord Seymour of Sudeley in 1547 but secretly and foolishly married Henry VIII's widow Catherine Parr, and died on the scaffold in 1549 having after Catherine's death attempted to marry the young Princess Elizabeth. The third child was his daughter Jane, who was married to Henry VIII on 30 May 1536, eleven days after the execution of Ann Boleyn. The birth of a son to Jane and her own death came after Sir John's own, but Edward and Thomas and others of their kin were to reap great rewards.

Jane Seymour, queen of Henry VIII (died 1537), after Holbein.

Lodge, i

No doubt thanks to his father's influence, Edward Seymour found employment early on in high places, serving Mary Tudor, Queen of France, in 1514, the Emperor Charles V before 1521, the Duke of Suffolk in 1523, the Duke of Richmond in 1525, Cardinal Wolsey in 1527 and the king himself in the 1530s. He was in the suite of the Archbishop of Canterbury at the coronation of Anne Boleyn in 1533. Soon after his sister's marriage to the king he was created Viscount Beauchamp, a title recalling his Somerset ancestor; and when the heir to the throne was also his nephew there came further rewards: the honour of carrying the Princess Elizabeth at Prince Edward's christening, the earldom of Hertford, the Garter, the offices of Lord High Admiral, Great Chamberlain of England and command of the army both on the Scottish border and in France.

And more. For a time was to come when Henry VIII was dead and the Earl of Hertford was uncle of the king, Governor of the king's person and Protector of the Realm, Treasurer of the Exchequer, Lord High Steward, Duke of Somerset, Earl Marshal of England, Captain-General within and without the Realm. These were no empty titles, but there were also material rewards including vast former monastic estates among which was the site and surrounding lands of Glastonbury Abbey, where the duke established a colony of Flemish weavers.

Edward Seymour, Duke of Somerset, Lord Protector (executed 1552), after Holbein.

Lodge, i

Such a man had enemies and in October 1549 he was deprived of his offices and sent to the Tower, where he stayed for nearly four months. A pardon and reinstatement were only temporary, for in October 1551 he was again in the Tower accused of high treason and felony. Three months later he was beheaded on Tower Hill and shortly afterwards his honours were forfeited. A modern verdict declares he had 'instincts of genuine statesmanship … one who brought his country at least one step nearer toleration and … liberty'.

The dukedom of Somerset was revived in 1660 in favour of a man who had fought gallantly for his king. William Seymour, great-grandson of Protector Somerset, began badly – or rather unwisely – by marrying a royal, namely Lady Arabella Stuart, the king's cousin. The marriage (he was twenty-two, she thirty-four) took place in her room at Greenwich Palace in June 1610 and His Majesty was displeased. Both were imprisoned, he in the Tower, she at Lambeth, and though both escaped she was recaptured and was kept in the Tower until her death, 'distracted', in 1615. Her aunt and accomplice the Countess of Shrewsbury was also imprisoned. (Incidentally, the bridegroom's grandfather, the Earl of Hertford, was also much displeased; he had been in similar trouble in 1560 for marrying Lady Katherine Grey.)

Lady Arabella Stuart, cousin of James I who clandestinely married William Seymour in 1610 and was punished with imprisonment in the Tower 1611 until her death in 1615; after Van Somer.

Lodge, i

William Seymour lived in France until his wife's death and was then allowed to return home and was forgiven. In 1621 he succeeded his grandfather as Earl of Hertford but took little part in public affairs, although he fought a duel in Marylebone Park in 1636 and had his opponent at his mercy until the park-keeper intervened. He was appointed joint Lord-Lieutenant of Somerset in 1639 and as King and Parliament began their collision course his sympathies were at first with Parliament. His appointment to the Privy Council and his promotion to be Marquess of Hertford indicated a change of heart and at the beginning of the Civil War he was Lieutenant-General of the South West and of South Wales. In 1643 he led the successful campaign which took Taunton, Bridgwater and Dunster and ended in the victory over Waller at Lansdown. Thereafter he remained close to the king, surrendering Oxford on his behalf. He was one of only four peers present at the king's funeral at Windsor, each one having (it is said) offered themselves for punishment in his place on the grounds that he had taken their advice.

William Seymour, Duke of Somerset (died 1660), after Vandyck.

Lodge, i

He was rewarded with the Garter while in exile in Jersey and at the Restoration again joined the Privy Council and became Lord-Lieutenant of both Somerset and Wiltshire. His greatest reward was the reversal of the attainder of his great-grandfather Edward and thus the restoration to him of the dukedom of Somerset. This 'man of great honour, great interest in fortune and estate, and of a universal esteem over the kingdom' enjoyed his new title for little more than a month and died at Great Bedwyn aged seventy-four, leaving as his heir his eight-year-old grandson and name-sake. The younger William, a student at Lincoln's Inn for less than a year, died in London of a malignant fever aged nineteen.

The next Duke of Somerset was the boy's uncle, the 5th and youngest son of old Duke William. He had been an MP, was a member of Gray's Inn, and Lord-Lieutenant of both Somerset and Wiltshire. His death without children in 1675 brought great benefit to poor children of Salibury, who received £300 for their apprenticeships, but the family faced yet another succession crisis. The new duke was Francis, a great-nephew of old Duke William and a first cousin once removed to the deceased. He did not last long; he died in 1678, shot at the door of an inn near Genoa. He was twenty and unmarried.

Again the succession was a close-run thing. The heir was his sixth and youngest brother Charles, a youth of sixteen and remembered for his extreme arrogance: 'a man', wrote Macaulay, 'in whom the pride of birth and rank amounted almost to a disease'. He was Lord-Lieutenant of Somerset from 1683 until dismissed by James II in 1687, and as such he led the Somerset militia (hardly successfully) against the Duke of Monmouth. He commanded the Queen's Regiment of Dragoons for two years but was relieved of this and other offices for refusing to introduce the Pope's nuncio at Windsor. He supported the Prince of Orange but was unable to vote that the throne was vacant. Early in Anne's reign he held government offices but never for long except the Mastership of the Horse 1702–12. Perhaps his most important political act was to burst into the meeting of the Privy Council, with the Duke of Argyll, on 30 July 1714, thereby ensuring the smooth succession of George I.

The duke's first marriage had wide-ranging dynastic consequences and explains why some of his papers are still to be found at Alnwick Castle and why the medieval cartulary of Athelney found its way (and has only just been rediscovered after more than two centuries) to Petworth House. His wife was the red-haired Elizabeth Percy ('Carrots from Northumberland', wrote Swift), not then sixteen and already twice widowed, the heiress of Joceline, Earl of Northumberland, and his vast estates including Alnwick and Petworth.

The proud duke died in 1748 and was followed by his second son Algernon who had served with distinction in the wars against the French, fighting as a volunteer at Oudenarde and on Marlborough's staff at Malplaquet. He rose to be a full General in 1747, served for more than four years as Governor of Minorca and, almost out of character, was a Fellow and from 1724–49 President of the Society of Antiquaries of London.

Charles Seymour, Duke of Somerset (the Proud Duke) (died 1748), after Kneller.

Lodge, i

Duke Algernon was already weighed down with titles but in 1744 his only son George died of smallpox in Bologna on his nineteenth birthday. In order that all should not be lost, he was in 1749 created Baron Warkworth and Earl of Northumberland with special remainder, should he himself have no male heir, to his son-in-law Sir Hugh Smithson; and on the next day he was created Baron Cockermouth and Earl of Egremont with special remainder to the children of his sister Lady Katherine, wife of Sir William Wyndham of Orchard. The duke had no further children, so at his death the barony of Percy passed to his daughter, and Sir Hugh Smithson and Sir Charles Wyndham received their respective titles. His Grace's titles of Earl of Hertford, Baron Beauchamp and Baron Seymour of Trowbridge became, for very good legal reasons, extinct and the dukedom of Somerset and the barony of Seymour passed to the Wiltshireman Sir Edward Seymour, his fifth cousin once removed.

There were eight dukes between the death of Duke Algernon in 1750 and the death of another Duke Algernon in 1923 including three brothers who died between 1885 and 1894. Had death duties been then invented, their 25,387 acres in eight counties (6553 in Somerset including Witham Friary)

116

worth £37,577 a year would have been seriously plundered. One of the eight was obsessed with the risks from smallpox after inoculation; one, of literary and scientific bent, who changed the spelling of his name to St Maur as if to suggest a greater antiquity but insisted on naming all his daughters Jane; one who held a number of government posts ending as First Lord of the Admiralty under Lord Palmerston; and the last who spent some of his youth as a rancher in Western America and was President of Dr Barnardo's Homes.

On the death of that last duke in 1923 without children four members of the family claimed the title and after deliberating on the proof of death of one John Hudson, a seaman, in India in 1786 and the consequent validity of the marriage of his widow, the daughter of a Woolwich publican to Colonel Francis Compton Seymour, the House of Lords declared in March 1925 that Brigadier-General Sir Edward Hamilton Seymour, a third cousin once removed of the last duke, should be his successor.

The present Duke of Somerset, who lives at the ancestral seat of Berry Pomeroy in Devon, is a chartered surveyor; his father and grandfather were both soldiers. He still owns land in Somerset and is patron of the living of Witham Friary as his ancestors before him.

◇◇◆◇◇

Smyth of Ashton Court

The Smyths (or Smiths or Smythes) came from Aylburton near Lydney in the Forest of Dean and settled in Bristol; Matthew (died 1526) was a merchant, his brother Thomas (died 1542) a hooper. Matthew's son John overtopped them both and the survival of one of his many account books among the family archives shows how. He made his money buying up cloth in Somerset and Wiltshire, leather from the Forest of Dean and from Wales, lead from the Mendips and local wheat, and then exporting them to France and Spain. And his own ship, the *Trinity* (worth £250), and those of his partners brought back oil and dyestuffs for the clothiers and wine, iron, fish and salt for anyone who would buy at a sensible price.

He was ever the merchant, keeping his counting house in Small Street until the day of his death, but he was also a public servant and a shrewd investor in land. He was sheriff of his native city once and mayor twice, and was instrumental in the city's purchase of former church land, but his own most significant purchase was made in 1545 when he bought Sir Thomas Arundell's estate at Long Ashton for the sum of £920. In the following year he bought another estate in the parish, formerly belonging to Bath Abbey, and by the time of his death in 1556, worth in cash and goods over £2263, he had land in Gloucestershire and more in Somerset. He was a gentleman, with a fine manor house, a coat of arms, a sister married to Thomas Phelips of Montacute (father of Sir Edward) and he sent his two sons to Oxford and the Inns of Court.

Trade, of course, was now forgotten; political and social alliance was the order of the day. Son Hugh married a Biccombe lady of West Somerset, represented Wareham in parliament in 1554 and died in 1580 leaving a daughter. Son Matthew's son Hugh married a daughter of Sir Thomas Gorges of Longford Castle and his daughter Anne married a Rodney – old blood and old money. Hugh, early in life something of a dandy, was later depressed, irritable and obsessed with his health. He was knighted in 1603, a recognition of his wealth. Two years later he was on an embassy to the Archduke of Austria, but evidently his disposition was against him and he was not employed again.

Sir Hugh Smyth (died 1627).
J. H. Bettey, *The Rise of a Gentry Family: the Smyths of Ashton Court* (Historical Assoc., Bristol Branch, 1978)

Three days before his own death in 1627 his eighteen-year-old son Thomas was married to Florence, eldest daughter of Lord Poulett, a move intended to preserve the Smyth estate from administration by the Court of Wards. It was a match which brought young Smyth into local Somerset politics, perhaps uncomfortably because as his father-in-law was the leading royalist, so his uncle Sir Robert Phelips was one of the leaders of the opposition in the House of Commons. Thomas, evidently an amiable man, served as JP and was elected for the county to the Short Parliament of 1640, failed at the election later in the same year, but was returned for Bridgwater in 1641. He was expelled for following the instructions of the Crown in August 1642 and immediately helped raise a troop of horse. For the first few months of the Civil War he was active for the king but, having marched from Sherborne Castle to Minehead and crossed to Cardiff, he contracted smallpox and died.

Thomas's son Hugh (1632–80) seems to have been a pragmatic politician; happy to conspire against the Protectorate and happy to serve as a magistrate under it. He sat in the Restoration Parliament, was made a Knight of the Bath and a baronet at Charles II's coronation. Like most of his class he was magistrate, sheriff, deputy lieutenant and royal commissioner, and stirred himself at new elections in 1679 when he and Sir John Sydenham were successful against two court candidates although he had voted against excluding the Catholic Duke of York from the succession and was thus considered 'doubtful' by the Whig leader.

Sir John's son and grandson both served as sheriff of the county, but when the latter died without children in 1741 the baronetcy held by the family became, for the first time, extinct. It was revived thanks to the second marriage of the younger John's sister Florence to another Smith of Bristol. Jarrit Smith, son of John Smith of the city, was created a baronet in 1763, and the title passed to his son John Hugh (died 1802) and to his two nephews in turn, Hugh (died 1824) and John (died 1849).

The heir to the estate in 1849 was the last baronet's elder sister Florence (died 1852 at the age of eighty-three), widow of John Upton, who adopted the name Smyth. Her grandson John Henry Greville Upton replaced Upton by Smyth on succeeding. Soon after he was faced with an unpleasant shock, for Sir Richard Hugh Smyth claimed both the estate and the title as son of the 3rd baronet. In the event the man proved to be a clever imposter, producing almost convincing family documents forged with the help of a former domestic servant at Ashton Court. The stakes were high, an estate worth £30,000 a year; the penalty for failure twenty years' transportation.

The genuine heir was created a baronet in 1859, the third in the family, but again the title died out on his death without children in 1901. Ashton Court and the estate, however, passed to his widow Emily Frances, who died in 1914. Her daughter by her first marriage was Esme, later wife of the Hon. Gilbert Neville Irby. They took the name Smyth on coming into the property and the Hon. Esme Smyth remained there until her death in 1946.

Florence, daughter of John, 1st Baron Poulett, wife of Thomas Smyth.
J. H. Bettey, *The Rise of a Gentry Family: the Smyths of Ashton Court* (Historical Assoc., Bristol Branch, 1978)

In the following year the house was stripped of its contents, including the huge family archive. The house and immediate park were bought by Bristol Corporation in 1959.

Ashton Court, Long Ashton, 1831; engraving by J. Brett after drawing by Henrietta Sheppard.

SAS

Speke of Whitelackington, Dillington and Rowlands

The woodpecker is undoubtedly a persistent bird, hammering away at massive timbers to make a large enough entrance for a home. The Speke family, formerly Espec, the French word for wood-pecker, has certainly been persistent, recorded in Normandy before the Conquest and in Devon in the twelfth century. Ever since the fifteenth, however, Spekes have lived in Somerset; and in 1702 they even sold the lordship of the place which still bears their name, Brampford Speke.

When John Speke of Heywood in Wembworthy in mid Devon married the Somerset heiress Joan Keynes in about 1420 he became, through her, owner of the manors of Compton Martin, Dowlishwake, West Dowlish, and Cudworth, and also of a manor in Hampshire. Twice he served as MP for his native county, beginning a tradition of political service which his descendants were to follow. Another tradition was service abroad, in his case in 1431 abroad in company with the king, in 1440 and 1441 in command of 300 troops patrolling the English Channel against the French. He captured an enemy carrack in August 1441 but died in early October, perhaps at sea. He was buried in the parish church of Dowlishwake.

Sir John, as by then he was, left the family in some turmoil and histori-ans with a slight problem. The turmoil was that debts and legacies amounted to £257 and the executors only had just over £89 in cash to pay them. The problem is that the will as copied into the register of Bishop Lacy was dated several days after he had died and remained unsettled for seven years, at least in part because two of his executors refused to serve. By that time there had been further family upset. Sir John's son and heir had died.

That second John had done two important things for the family. Like his father he had married a Somerset heiress, Alice Beauchamp, heiress of the manors of Whitelackington and Atherstone, conveniently adjoining Dowlishwake; and by her he had a son, another John. But the younger John was obviously a minor and the family finances were clearly in some disorder. No wonder his grandfather's will remained unproved.

The third John Speke kept a foot both in Devon and Somerset. In his early years he was probably brought up in the Courtenay household at Tiverton Castle, and when he came of age he lived either at Haywood or at Dowlishwake, but after his mother's death he moved to Whitelackington. He sat for Somerset in the Parliament of 1478 but was an elector in Devon; he was a JP in Somerset and Wiltshire. His knighthood may have been tactfully accepted in return for a cash donation to the king; the £200 fine Henry VII levied on him in 1497 may have reflected Sir John's reluctance to get involved on either side when the Cornish rebelled in favour of Perkin Warbeck.

In 1501 he was one of the local knights assigned to escort Catherine of Aragon through Somerset on her way to marry the heir to the throne, and was politically more active under that heir's brother, the new king Henry VIII. He had to provide 25 soldiers in 1512, was on board the *James* of Dartmouth in 1513 and served as sheriff of Devon in 1516–17. There was, however, another side to both him and his grandfather. The older John wanted 1000 masses to be said immediately after his death and 1000 annually thereafter, requested the prayers of the nuns of Polsloe and the Dominican and Franciscan friars of Exeter, arranged for annual commemorations in the churches of Brampford Speke, Wembworthy, Dowlishwake and Compton Martin, and left land to endow chantries for 100 years in the churches of Brampford Speke and Wembworthy. The chaplain at Wembworthy was also to celebrate mass three times a week in the Speke chapel at the manor house at Haywood.

The younger John received the equivalent of a passport to go to Rome on pilgrimage in 1467, a permission renewed in 1473 when the journey was more likely made. In his later years he was the friend and associate of Exeter clergy including three bishops and in 1518 he founded a chantry in the cathedral in the chapel of St George he had already built at the eastern end of the north choir aisle and matching the chapel of his friend Bishop Oldham on the south side. There, surrounded by the carved emblems of his friends as well as the double eagle of his own coat of arms, he was buried at his death in 1518. His widow Elizabeth joined him later.

None of this is mentioned in Sir John's will, drawn up while the chapel was being built. That is a more human document which reveals a man with a divided family. His eldest son, John, had evidently gone to live at Haywood, not just because he was the son and heir but also because he did not get on with his father's third wife; he may even have favoured his second son, named George after his favourite saint. So, should John the younger oppose the lands settled on his stepmother, he would lose the lands he had already been given and would also lose half the chain his father had been prepared to share between him and George. George, on the other hand, was to receive 200 marks (£133.33p) in cash, half his father's best chain and new tapestry hangings and coverlet.

Sir John's widow did not outlive her husband for long, and in her will revealed that the family quarrel continued: stepson George claimed that two little gold chains had belonged to his father. Should he successfully acquire them, then her cousin John would have to do without one and his wife would have to be content with a rope of pearls with a gold bead-stone instead.

The younger John died in 1524 leaving his son Thomas under age and his brother George as head of the family. George served as sheriff of Somerset as befitted a man of his rank and family tradition in 1526–7 and died in the later part of 1528. He too was deeply concerned for his soul, requesting 3000 masses at the time of his death and establishing a chantry in the new north aisle of Dowlishwake church including a weekly mass of St George. He wanted some silver candlesticks and basins to be given to his father's chapel at Exeter Cathedral and requested burial at Dowlishwake in a tomb to be shared with his wife 'with our pictures thereupon of copper … in scripture of copper who lieth there'. The brass still lies in the north chapel at Dowlishwake but Sir George is alone.

Monumental brass to Sir George Speke (died 1528), Dowlishwake church.

A. B. Connor, *Monumental Brasses in Somerset* (1970), 294

By the time of Sir George's death the family feud was almost healed. Thomas was to have his uncle's best gold chain with eighty-six links, presumably including that part which should have been his father's; and half the family plate; and, after his aunt's death, the other half of the plate, furniture and farm stock, always provided that he did nothing to alter his uncle's dispositions. Should he do so he would receive nothing.

Thomas was not so foolish as to object, and what he inherited when he came of age in the year following his uncle's death was a substantial fortune, considerably enhanced when his aunt died. For a few years what he did is not recorded, but from 1532 he began his career on the county bench of magistrates which only ended with his death. A stay in Calais early in 1535 with his friend Viscount Lisle showed he had friends of substance and in 1538 he was knighted. In the following year he was both pricked as sheriff and elected as county MP.

And now the local gentleman began a career at Court starting in a modest way to profit from work at the Augmentations Office which dealt with the disposal of the land of dissolved monasteries. He was appointed chief steward of the lands of Glastonbury Abbey, and was also an official of that part of the royal household with clear access to the king. He and his brother-in-law Sir Maurice Berkeley each received legacies of 200 marks (£166.33p) under the king's will. In 1544 he followed the family military tradition, serving in France with a troop of horse, and in the following year was permitted to have 40 servants all wearing his livery. Another royal post was certainly all for show: he was one of the challengers at tournaments held in honour of Edward VI's coronation.

In July 1551 several royal courtiers were struck down with the 'sweating sickness' and Sir Thomas was one of them. He died within two days and was buried in St Dunstan's in the West just outside the city of London though at least under the patronage of a Somerset saint. His widow did not receive the £240 'in old gold' and a life interest in East Dowlish because of her adultery.

After such flamboyance some becoming modesty. Sir Thomas's son George was made a Knight of the Bath at Elizabeth's coronation and was put on the county bench. He was sheriff in 1562–3 and just once sat for the county in parliament, between 1576 and 1581. He had friends enough, including William Herbert, Earl of Pembroke, owner of an estate not far from his own at Donyatt, for whom he stood as a character witness before the Privy Council. One of his prized possessions was a stone jug covered with silver which the Countess of Pembroke had given to him.

Sir George died in 1584 and was followed in succession by two more Georges, equally modest men, the first sensibly marrying a daughter of Sir John Portman and properly serving as sheriff of his native county in 1592–3. He died in 1637 when his heir was still a teenager. The younger George travelled abroad like a good Speke in 1639 and two years later married the daughter of the man who controlled his estates during his minority. His wife Mary Pye was an ardent Presbyterian and was related to that dangerous politician John Hampden.

George was not then inclined to politics but thought the king's camp at Bridgwater was the best place to be in 1645 and was fined £2390, much more than a year's income. When the king came back he was considered entirely loyal and served as sheriff in 1661–2, but began to incline to his wife's opinions. From 1663 he was no longer a magistrate and openly voiced the opinion that the king was ruled by his mistresses and the bishops were disloyal and popishly inclined. There was much sympathy for his stand and he was elected to parliament in 1679 and 1681.

He was, of course, under suspicion of treason, the 'old rebel' who openly entertained the Duke of Monmouth and a vast crowd of people at Whitelackington in 1680. The house was searched for arms at least once, his son Hugh and son-in-law John Trenchard, the Whig leader in Somerset, were charged with treason and he himself was arrested in 1685 for helping Trenchard to escape. Unlike his sons Charles and John he was thus not directly implicated in the Monmouth rebellion but his fine of £5000 was paid to secure a pardon for the remaining members of his family, Charles having been hanged at Ilminster because Lord Chief Justice Jeffreys declared the family owed a life. When William of Orange arrived George joined him, but died early in 1689, the only acknowledgement of his long adherence to the Whig cause being his appointment as a deputy lieutenent of his native county.

James Scott, Duke of Monmouth (executed 1685).

Lodge, ix

Like father like son; John Speke was lucky not to have faced Jeffreys in court, for he had joined Monmouth at Chard 'with a company of ragged horse' and became their colonel. He left the rebel army at Frome; some say he was dismissed for cowardice and went abroad. His collaboration with his father-in-law Edmund Prideaux would probably have been enough to condemn him. Even before the rebellion he had been implicated with his brother Hugh in the Popish Plot and sat in the two exclusion parliaments of 1679 as a member for Ilchester and for a short time was a deputy lieutenant. In 1688 he was more sympathetic to James II, uncertain about William of Orange and failed to win the trust of the Ilchester electors again.

However, by 1691 he was forgiven and was a deputy lieutenant once more and he sat as MP for Taunton between 1690 and 1698 as a Whig. After that his son George took up his political mantle, failing to be elected for the county in 1715 but serving continuously, first for Milborne Port and later for Taunton and Wells between 1722 and 1747. He normally supported Sir Robert Walpole's administration, once declaring himself reluctantly in favour of a motion to retain a standing army as a sick man takes medicine, 'necessary, though very bitter in going down and disagreeable to the palate'.

George was a wealthy man and married three times. At his death in 1753 he left two daughters. Mary, the elder, living unmarried at Sowton in Devon, was given £10,000 and was her father's heir. Anne, married to the later Whig Prime Minister Lord North, received land worth more than

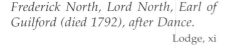

Frederick North, Lord North, Earl of Guilford (died 1792), after Dance.

Lodge, xi

£4000 a year and the house at Dillington which her grandfather had probably built and which became their home.

Where now was a male heir to carry on the line? George, the 'old rebel' had had five sons, but only John had issue. The male heir in 1753 was a descendant of the 'old rebel's' second son William, who had died in 1680. He was, in fact, another William and his great-grandson.

The new heir was about twenty when he took his place in his family's illustrious line and, like many before him, took on the responsibilities of a landowner rather earlier in life than he might have wished. Again, like many before him, he was sheriff in 1819–20, and was a deputy lieutenant. His marriage to a Dickinson of Kingweston allied him to one of the leaders of local politics. The house at Jordans replaced an earlier one in 1796 and was the first Speke house which might be called a mansion yet still retaining a modesty so characteristic of the family.

Jordans, Ashill, built 1796, demolished after 1958. Wash drawing by J. Buckler, 1832.

SAS

William Speke died in 1839 and was followed by his son, also William, whose marriage to Georgina, daughter of his neighbour William Hanning of Dillington, brought a new name to the family. The second William was a magistrate and a deputy lieutenant in the family tradition. His eldest son and successor in 1887 held the same offices and was the model Victorian country gentleman. The other sons reflected the Victorian age abroad, the age of Empire and exploration. The third son, Edward, died in Delhi; the second, John Hanning, though he died tragically near home in 1864, had served in the Indian Army and, in two expeditions to Central Africa, had discovered the headwaters of the Nile. His tomb in Dowlishwake church was the family's own tribute; his distraught father was permitted to add supporters to his coat of arms in acknowledgment of John's achievement.

William Speke, John Hanning's brother, died in 1908 and was succeeded by his nephew Walter Hanning Speke, sheriff of Somerset in 1927–8. Walter's next brother Gerald died in East Africa early in the 1920s without children; his youngest brother William had settled in South Africa and on Walter's death unmarried in 1944 he became the head of the family. By that time his own son, also William, was dead, killed in action in 1941. The heir presumptive in 1944 was Peter Gerald Hanning Speke, a schoolboy living in Toronto.

Peter came to Somerset as head of the family in 1965. Some of the ancestral lands had long been sold, Jordans had been demolished, but he and his family have made their home not very far away in the early-sixteenth-century former farmhouse called Rowlands. He is lord of the manors of Dowlishwake and Ashill and patron of the living of Curry Rivel. In true family tradition he serves on the bench of magistrates, was sheriff of the county in 1982–3 and is a deputy lieutenant, ready to help defend Somerset from invasion. And, as chairman of the trustees of Glastonbury Abbey, he has care of a Somerset monument which has an even longer history than his own.

Above: *Peter Speke, sheriff 1982-3; photograph by D. J. Wheadon.*

P. G. H. Speke, Esq

Right: *John Hanning Speke, 1863; engraving by S. Hollyer after photograph by Southwell Bros.*

J. H. Speke, *Journal of the Discovery of the Source of the Nile* (1863)

Stawell of Cothelstone

They were Somerset folk through and through, and the heralds who conducted the 1623 visitation were somehow convinced that they could trace their ancestry back eleven generations from the Sir Geoffrey who died in 1361, unlikely unless many died very young, and unlikely, too, because some of the names are not to be found in any contemporary documents. But their earliest known ancestors were probably that Geoffrey of Stawell who held a knight's fee at Stawell of the abbot of Glastonbury in 1189, and also that Geoffrey of Coveston or Cothelstone who held that estate in 1166.

Geoffrey was the favourite family name in the early years and there were at least five in the period up to 1340. The modest manor house at the foot of the Quantocks was the family's principal home, but the marriage of Sir John Stawell to Elizabeth Hext in the early-seventeenth century took them also to Low Ham where one of Sir John's sons spent money his father lost. Yet such was the esteem in which the family was held that Mary, the daughter and sole heir of the last Baron Stawell, was herself created a baroness with her father's title of Stawell of Somerton. By then, however, the family's Somerset estates had all been sold and she and her descendants lived first in Hampshire and subsequently in Gloucestershire.

The first prominent public figure in the family was Sir Thomas, son of Sir Matthew, who was born about 1369 and who died in 1439. In 1419, two years after military service abroad, local justices of the peace were asked by the king's council to name the men of the county best able and sufficient to do service in the defence of the realm. Thomas was second on the list, and it may be no surprise that in the next year he should have been elected an

Tomb of Sir Matthew Stawell (died 1379), Cothelstone church.

SASP lxvii

MP for the county. He was, however, never a JP but often sat on royal commissions in the following years, and was sheriff of Devon in 1434–5, a county where he had inherited land through his mother. Most of his energy, however, seems to have been spent either trying to prove his claim to the great estates of the Columbers family through his great-grandmother or serving Glastonbury Abbey where, after his death in 1439, he was buried among the abbots in the abbey church.

Sir Thomas was followed by his grandson Robert, who according to his will of 1499, wished to be buried in his parish church at Cothelstone and left to Robert Stawell the vestments, silver and service books of his private chapel and to Robert's son Edward a silver covered bowl called 'le Michael'. Stawells were unlucky with their sons: a grandson succeeded again in 1506, 1541 and 1604. The last was Sir John, the most royalist of royalists, who appears to have outlived all but three of his eleven children, many of whom followed the same political cause and suffered in consequence. John the eldest fought for the king but later went mad and was thus disinherited; Sir Edward, the second, equally ardent, went into exile in France and died in 1653; George, the third, inherited on his father's death in 1662 and rebuilt Low Ham church both as a mausoleum for his grandparents and a bold statement of his political and religious beliefs, but died without sons in 1669; Thomas, the fourth, probably died abroad. The rest disappeared almost without trace.

Monument to Sir John Stawell (died 1603), Cothelstone church; wash drawing by W. W. Wheatley, 1844.

SAS

Sir John Stawell, the royalist father, was MP for Somerset in Charles I's first parliament and 'employed himself heartily' in the matter of a forced loan for the king in 1626, making himself unpopular with his neighbours. He was sheriff in the county in 1628–9 and an active JP, which then meant someone who was prepared during the period when Charles I dispensed with parliament to carry out government orders. He was a generous subscriber to the fund to send troops to Scotland in 1639 and two years later he was chosen with Sir John Poulett to be a member of what came to be called the Long Parliament. Both men were expelled after nine months for, with Sir Ralph Hopton and Lord Hertford, Stawell had begun raising men back home. He was leader of the troops who won the skirmish at Marshalls Elm, between Street and Compton Dundon, the first action of the Civil War in the county.

Soon Somerset was no place for a leading royalist and Sir John retreated with Hopton to Pendennis Castle in Cornwall, but when the king's fortunes recovered Sir John was appointed governor of Taunton in 1643. He was in Exeter when the final surrender was made in 1646 but unlike many of his fellows he would not compromise, refusing to promise not to resist religious changes proposed by the government nor to assist the king, typical of the man who was later said to have made himself obnoxious to Parliament. As a result he was committed first to Ely House and later to Newgate and was tried for treason. He spent the next four years in gaol and was then removed to the Tower and tried by a special court. The court would not pass sentence but his estates were sold and £7000 of the proceeds were given to Taunton to compensate for war damage. Some thought him a 'lofty, proud man'; others, even political opponents, felt his punishment to be harsh. He remained in the Tower until 1653 and then was kept in London, living on a pension of £6 a week, until early in 1660.

Of course he came back to power at the Restoration. He was among those who welcomed Charles II at Charing Cross, and his estates, terribly damaged by their erstwhile owners, were restored to him. He reckoned his losses were over £30,000. He returned to the county bench of magistrates, again served as deputy lieutenant and was elected to parliament, but he died early in 1662 and the pomp of his funeral at Cothelstone has probably never been matched in the county. The cortège started out from Low Ham, rested overnight at Bishop's Lydeard, and came at last to Cothelstone, led by two conductors, two trumpeters, the bailiffs of his twenty-three manors and heralds bearing all the trappings of chivalry. Thus passed a man of 'eminent courage and fidelity', known to some as 'a great chymist' because his concern for his health led him never to eat breakfast in order to clean his stomach before dinner. His end was, perhaps, more show than substance; the family was already in a precarious position and Sir John's sons and grandson were finally to destroy it. Sir John's final victory, which he would surely have relished, was the hanging at Cothelstone of Richard Bovett, colonel of the Duke of Monmouth's Taunton (Blue) regiment; that same Richard Bovett, colonel of the Somerset militia under Cromwell, who had been the none-too-careful sequestrator of the property and treated Lady Stawell harshly when Sir John languished in captivity.

George Stawell, Sir John's third but first surviving son, was sheriff in 1666–7 and died in 1669, the year in which Low Ham church was consecrated. His brother Ralph, an even greater Anglican zealot, commanded the Bridgwater militia regiment and with its physical power behind him

Tombs of Ralph, Baron Stawell (died 1689) and John, 2nd Baron Stawell (died 1692), Low Ham church.

G. D. Stawell, *A Quantock Family* (1910)

was active against Dissenters. He served as sheriff in 1676–7 and for a short time from 1679 was a Tory MP for Bridgwater. Early in 1683 he was raised to the peerage as Baron Stawell of Somerton, a recognition of the sacrifice his father had made in the royalist cause; and his continued loyalty to the Crown found him leading his men against the Duke of Monmouth. His shame when they all deserted ran deep. As a desperate measure James II appointed him Lord-Lieutenant in place of the Catholic Lord Waldegrave in November 1688, but Lord Stawell's loyalty knew some bounds and he soon joined the Prince of Orange. He did not retain his office under the new régime and died in the summer of 1689 at the age of forty-eight.

Lord Stawell, like his brother George, was buried at Low Ham where both had made their home. His heir was his son John, the 2nd baron, who had probably joined the Prince of Orange before his father and spent some time in Amsterdam before his early death in 1692, leaving only one daughter. So the title passed to John's half-brother William, who served as Gentleman of the Bedchamber to Prince George of Denmark, Queen Anne's husband. His only son and heir, another William, died at Marseilles in 1740 and he himself died two years later also leaving an only daughter. The title then passed to his childless only surviving brother Edward, who early in his career had travelled abroad for the government and who in 1712 was Comptroller of the Lottery. Lord Stawell died of apoplexy at his home at Hinton Ampner in Hampshire in 1755 and is said to have haunted the place for some years.

The 2nd Baron Stawell had been buried at Low Ham, the 3rd baron at Hartley Wespall, for the old Hext family house at Low Ham had been largely pulled down to make way for a huge mansion with a frontage of 400 feet, which seems to have been started by the 2nd baron in the 1680s. An account book begun by him and continued by his son records spending

John Stawell, 2nd Baron Stawell (died 1692), artist unknown.

G. D. Stawell, *A Quantock Family* (1910)

Low Ham, barn incorporating remains of the Stawell mansion, c. 1870. The arch now forms part of the entrance arch to Hazlegrove House, near Sparkford.

SAS

on workmen's wages until the end of 1691 but also on flower seeds, melon glasses, orange trees, a duck decoy, a pair of battledores and three shuttle-cocks 'for the young ladies', the second part of Dryden's 'Absalom and Achitophel', 'several' pictures by Mr Cufund and a payment of £20 to the painter Griffier, presumably to record one of his famous bird's-eye views of the emerging house and the vast terraced garden. The house was never finished and the whole estate was sold by the 3rd Lord Stawell to pay his vast debts; small wonder, for the account book also records half-yearly payments of £150 (usually late) to Child the London banker, £1500 to Colonel Berkeley and similar large sums towards the £30,000 which had been settled in 1681 on Ursula, daughter of the late George Stawell when she became the third wife of Edward, Earl of Conway. The whole sum was never found for the earl died in 1683, but his memory lived on. Not until the summer of 1686 were the windows in the church mended which Conway had broken. The church still remains in a field where once Lord Stawell grew African and French marigolds and larkspur below a terraced garden designed by Jacob Bobart before a house for which the architect William Taylor may have supplied the design.

◇◇◆◇◇

Stuckey of Langport

Businessmen, not landed gentry; but as bankers throughout the county and beyond they could well have provided the means for gentlemen to be gentlemen. The American branch of the family likes to think they have Dutch origins; other Stuckeys believed they came from medieval Devon. Somerset origins are definitely in Kingsdon in the 1570s with an unbroken link from George Stuckey, baptised in the parish church there in 1665.

From Kingsdon George moved a few miles west where he had set up in Langport as a worsted comber by 1699 – a common enough trade in this clothmaking country – and later became a serge maker. The town he settled in prospered thanks to the easy movement of goods along the Parrett between Ilchester, the county town, and Bridgwater, Somerset's largest port. In the later fifteenth century woad for dyers had come over-land from Southampton for distribution throughout the county. Trade patterns had changed by the seventeenth century but Somerset cloth was still in demand and the flat-bottomed barges of Langport still plied along the river to the Langport Slip by Bridgwater's bridge.

George's son, also George, was described as a merchant, which probably meant he had fingers in most businesses along the river; and he went into a fruitful partnership with Thomas Bagehot, a maltster, who had arrived in the town by 1747. Together those two entrepreneurs touched anything that moved on the Parrett, bulk goods so much cheaper to transport by water such as grain, timber, coal and salt.

George Stuckey died in 1774 and was followed, as in gentry families, by his son George (died 1807), also a merchant; Thomas Bagehot was followed by his son Robert Codrington Bagehot (died 1836). But George had another son Samuel, who had other ideas. In about 1770 he used his family's money to establish a bank in Langport. By 1826, when it had branches in Bristol and Bridgwater, it became a joint stock company with Vincent Stuckey (died 1845), youngest son of the third George, as its chairman. He was, besides being an astute businessman, both nephew and son-in-law of the founder, and in his youth he had been private secretary at the Treasury to both William Pitt the younger and William Huskisson.

During the nineteenth century the bank absorbed thirteen others, mostly local, and there was not a town in the county which did not have a branch of Stuckeys in its main street and its manager a man of importance in the community. Vincent's grandson Vincent Wood, chairman in his turn until 1900, was proud to add Stuckey to his name, just as many an heir to landed estates changed his in order to inherit. The bank was absorbed by Parr's Bank in 1909, at a time when its banknote circulation was second only to that of the Bank of England. The final successor to this financial genealogy was the NatWest. Stuckey and Bagehot continued to trade. Before the French Revolution they were sending goods by water and road to Birmingham, Manchester, Liverpool and London. By 1866 they are said to have owned a fleet of fourteen East Indiaman and nineteen barges. The Somerset Trading Company, as it came to be known, had tentacles everywhere.

The family continued, of course, and in two generations after Vincent Stuckey in the female line produced two men of national stature. One was

Walter Bagehot, economist (died 1877); portrait by Adolphe Beau.
SAS

Walter Bagehot, son of Vincent's youngest sister Edith. Walter (1826–77) was an economist and a journalist. He was educated in Bristol and at University College, London. He won medals for his intellectual brilliance, was called to the bar and in 1852 he joined the family firm. From 1872 he was deputy recorder of Langport Corporation and lived at Herd's Hill House, just outside the town. His greatest contribution was his service as editor of the *Economist* from 1860 until his death in 1877 and his book entitled *The English Constitution*. Among his greatest admirers was Woodrow Wilson, who rode over to Langport in 1896 to visit his grave beside the parish church.

The other was Vincent Stratton Stuckey Coles. Vincent Stuckey's daughter Eliza married James Stratton Coles, a clergyman who was rector of Shepton Beauchamp from 1836 until his death in 1872. James Coles revolutionised the parish, introducing daily Matins, frequent communion services and weekday sermons. He was succeeded in 1872 by his son Vincent Stratton Stuckey Coles, who stayed as parish priest for only two years, but whose connection with Shepton continued until his death in 1929.

The Revd. V. S. S. Coles (died 1929). Photograph by Guillman, c.1898.

Stuckey Coles was a leader of the Tractarian movement, a popular preacher in the United States as well as all over England, a hymn writer and trainer of clergy. From 1884 he was based in Oxford, where he was Warden of Pusey House from 1897 until 1909. He used his family inheritance in many ways; in Shepton in the building of two houses, one as a home for himself which his sister later used as a home to provide training in laundry and housework 'for the reception of young girls who have fallen', the other a house for a group of celibate clergymen. Coles also put money into the publication of *English Hymnal*. A biographer described him as a man whose 'spiritual power influenced not Oxford only but penetrated the whole Anglican Communion'.

◇◇ ◆ ◇◇

Trevelyan of Nettlecombe

They liked to believe that the mythical land of Lyonesse gave them birth and that a white horse saved one of them by swimming with its master to safety on the Cornish mainland when their former home sank beneath the sea. Perhaps solid Cornish yeoman origins were not imaginative enough in the seventeenth century and a white horse incorporated in the family's coat of arms gave the idea of dashing possibilities. But in truth the Trevelyans were yeomen farmers from the farm of the same name in the parish of St Veep not far from Fowey; and they were there in the thirteenth century.

The Cornish chough might have been a more historically correct symbol to have taken, for it was the nickname given to that John Trevelyan who made his name, married wealth and settled in Somerset at Nettlecombe. The name, though, was one of hatred and derision, for like many another he had been too enthusiastic for Lancaster and paid the penalty of Lancastrian failure. The adherents of Jack Cade in 1450 accused him of 'blinding' the king and since 1441 he had certainly held household offices under Henry VI through which lucrative offices were available in his native Cornwall – steward of the duchy, keeper of Trematon Castle, parker of Restormel, keeper of the fishery at Fowey – as well as such posts as keeper of the armoury in the Tower of London, and constable of Hadley Castle. Such a man was needed to ensure Crown strength in parliament, and he was returned on at least three elections, in 1453–4 for the county of Cornwall. His influence, of course, depended on the effectiveness of the king and he was denounced in parliament and removed from his offices. He recovered his position for a few years but the fall of Lancaster in 1460 spelled the fall of Trevelyan. When Henry VI returned to power in 1470–1 Trevelyan lay low, and it was left to his eldest son to rise against the Yorkists in 1484 in the person of Richard III. Henry Tudor's victory at Bosworth brought father and son back into the political fold.

John Trevelyan and his Somerset heiress Elizabeth Whalesborough had at least seven sons of whom the eldest was made a Knight of the Bath when Arthur, Prince of Wales, married Catherine of Aragon in 1501. Two others had posts at court. Sir John, who had succeeded his father in 1492, died in 1522 and his elder son, another John, succeeded him. That John was later said to have been 'not the wisest man, nor yet of a surety no idiot, but a man of little discretion'. To have married his son, another John, into the Hill family and to have let Nettlecombe to John Sydenham and his family turned out to have been acts of foolishness.

He died in 1546, and successive Johns died in 1563 (having fathered twelve children) and 1577. Younger sons seem to have cost the family estate dear, but the next John Trevelyan, who married into the Chichester and Courtenay family, managed to find enough money to rebuild the family home. The hall and porch of the present house are dated 1599.

Nettlecombe Court and church; wash drawing, artist unknown and undated.

SAS

If the house was something of a triumph, some members of the family were not. John's brother William was sent off to serve first with Sir Francis Drake and later with Sir George Sydenham rather than be allowed to continue his career as a cattle and sheep rustler. More respectable was his son George who, enjoying the patronage of his Chichester uncle the Lord Deputy Governor in Ireland, became the first MP for Belfast and a knight. Another son, Christopher, was a perpetual student at Oxford; the eldest, another John, died just before his father, leaving nine-year-old George to the mercies of his not-very-satisfactory uncle Amias.

George Trevelyan was for the king in the Civil War like his mother's brother Thomas Luttrell, but his loyalty cost him very dear. He served under Sir Ralph Hopton and was commissioned to raise a foot regiment of 1200 men; his notion to put his colours on their coats was frowned on. Already in debt and with eleven children to support, George was nevertheless treated viciously and was required in 1646 to find £1560, a task made no easier because his house had been plundered, first in 1643 by a mob led by the rector of the parish, a staunch Parliamentarian, and later more effectually by Parliamentary troops. A year later a second fine was imposed and his lands confiscated. The fine was not fully paid until 1649 and by that time he had lost his wife. He himself died, no doubt a broken man, in 1653.

A grateful king could not undo the wrong, but in 1662 George's son, another George, was created a baronet as a reward for his father's service and sacrifice. His marriage to Mary Willoughby brought him the prospect of profitable estates in Devon, but he was evidently the butt of Sir William Wyndham's humour because of his sobriety – hardly the gay cavalier of the time. He too died young and his heir, his third and only surviving son, was only a year old.

Sir John Trevelyan (1670–1755) took on the public duties which most of his family had shunned since the time of their great ancestor in the fifteenth century. He was returned to parliament for Somerset in 1695 and 1701, and for Minehead four times until 1722. He was sheriff in 1704–5. In 1721 he was thought to be a leading Jacobite, perhaps because his fellow member for Minehead was Sir William Wyndham. Sir John's main concern was to defend the future of his estate from the likely depredations of his profligate son and heir. Sir George did, indeed, manage to do great damage in the few years of his control, but that damage was more than repaired in the time of his son, another Sir John, who married the daughter of a wealthy London merchant and inherited from his uncle, Sir Walter Blackett, estates in Northumberland and Durham. With the estates went his uncle's parliamentary seat at Newcastle-upon-Tyne, which he held for a few years until he was returned for Somerset between 1780 and 1796. Much earlier, in 1768, he had set up in opposition to Sir Charles Kemeys Tynte, but failed to get the support of Richard Hippisley Coxe and had been forced to withdraw. In the 1780s he usually voted with the opposition and was a supporter of Pitt (and named a son after him), but gout often prevented him from attending and voting. His popularity in the county meant that his election costs were always low, and he was remembered as 'a gentleman beloved and revered in every domestic and social relation'. Moves by his son and political allies to acquire a peerage for him (the Prime Minister, Spencer Perceval, was his son's brother-in-law) came to nothing, perhaps because of his own lack of enthusiasm. Politics for him, it seems, had been a matter of form; his real concern was to improve his estates, rebuild farmsteads and embellish his house and park at Nettlecombe. He died in 1828 at the age of ninety-two, outliving all but two of his children.

The next baronet, another John, found himself with divided loyalties, for his wife infinitely preferred to live at Wallington in Northumberland, no

Sir John Trevelyan (died 1755).
Bush and Corbett,'Nettlecombe Court'

matter what improvements he made at Nettlecombe; and the same applied to his son, Sir Walter Calverley Trevelyan, who succeeded in 1846. Father and son were of a different mould from their ancestors, the father interested in science, music and education, the son a naturalist and antiquarian, and passionately interested in the cause of temperance. Sir Walter and his wife Pauline made Wallington something of an artistic mecca, entertaining Ruskin, Holman Hunt and others. Nettlecombe remained in the capable hands of local agents John and James Babbage.

On the death of Sir Walter without children in 1879 (his fine cellar was bequeathed to a doctor 'to be applied to scientific purposes') there came a parting of the ways. Wallington, with family portraits and china, went to his cousin Sir Charles Trevelyan, who had married Lord Macaulay's sister and who had served in India and at the Treasury; Wallington's furniture, Nettlecombe and the baronetcy passed to another cousin, Alfred, who had lived in Ireland for most of his life and who had upset Sir Walter by becoming a Roman Catholic. Sir Alfred, evidently a most charitable man, died without male heirs in 1891 and Nettlecombe and the title passed to a Cornish cousin Walter.

Sir W. J. Trevelyan (died 1931) as sheriff of Cornwall 1906-7.

Mates

Sir Walter Trevelyan was a thorough countryman, establishing the Nettlecombe Harriers in 1895 and supporting the West Somerset Foxhounds. He served as sheriff of Cornwall in 1906–7. At his death in 1931 there came a further parting of the ways; his only son Willoughby John succeeded to the title and supporting estates, but Nettlecombe passed to his only surviving daughter Joan, later the wife of the painter Garnet Ruskin Wolseley. Willoughby John, the 9th baronet, died unmarried in 1976 and was followed by a Californian distant cousin, whose son, Edward Norman Trevelyan, the 11th baronet, succeeded in 1996. He won a gold medal for yachting in the 1984 Olympics and works as an administrator at the University of California. Wallington has been in the hands of the National Trust since 1958; Nettlecombe Court was a girls' school in the early 1960s and, since 1967, has been the Leonard Wills Field Studies Centre, but the estate still belongs to the Wolseley family.

$$\diamond\diamond\blacklozenge\diamond\diamond$$

Vaughan-Lee of Dillington

he Vaughan-Lees were unusual; the Vaughan was Welsh, the Lee
was from Devon, but to begin with (well, not to begin with in the
strictest sense because where and how they began is beyond the
author's knowledge) they were Hannings, prosperous Somerset yeomen
farmers. The marriage of John Hanning of Dillington to Susan Harvard of
Whitelackington, daughter of Thomas Harvard of Thorney, is the acknowledged beginning of the family pedigree. John's interest in the estate at
Dillington formerly belonging to the Spekes and after them to the earls of
Guilford had begun by 1794 and in the following year he put down the
huge sum of £52,000, raised by a mortgage on Barrington Court, then little
more than a crumbling farmhouse. The sum was probably not immediately forthcoming, and the Trent family (who might well have provided
some of the money) continued to be involved, but John could consider
himself owner of Dillington House in 1799, though the complete purchase
money was now said to be £83,000.

John's son William evidently and fortunately married money. His bride in
1800 was Harriet Lee of Pinhoe, and a son, John Lee Hanning was born to
them in 1802. Five years later grandfather John Hanning died, intestate, at
what was then known as Whitelackington House and now
Whitelackington Manor. Little more than five months later Harriet
Hanning was also dead, leaving behind her son John and two daughters.
There was probably no compensation for the loss of his mother, but his
uncle Major Edward Lee, of Orleigh Court in Devon, died unmarried in
1819 leaving him a substantial estate provided he changed his name to Lee.
This he did on achieving his majority in 1822. Probably it was this circum-
stance which allowed his father William finally to shake off the Trent family
in 1826, making him the undisputed owner of the entire Dillington estate
which the Spekes had held for so long. And, curiously, just two years
before, William's daughter Georgina married William Speke of Jordans.

William Hanning had become interested, personally and financially, in the
Gurney Steam Carriage Company, then based in London, applying steam
power to roads as it was being applied to rails. The company collapsed in
1832 with considerable financial loss, and William himself died in 1834.

John Lee Lee was, of course, financially secure thanks to his uncle; and he was by then an MP, elected for Wells in 1831 and representing the city until 1837. In 1845–6 he served as sheriff. In 1834 he married Jessy, the daughter of the late John Edwards Vaughan of Rheola and Llanelay, near Neath, a man who like himself had changed his name.

John Lee Lee (died 1874), rebuilder of Dillington House.

N. Smith, *The Story of Dillington: A Thousand Years* (2000)

John Edwards Vaughan had been born John Edwards; his grandfather had moved to Glamorgan from Staffordshire (but surely of Welsh origin) and his father had bought Rheola in 1800. John Edwards himself was born in London and made money as a parliamentary solicitor, as solicitor to the Regents Canal Company, and as agent to several noblemen; he was a near relative to the fashionable architect John Nash. His return as MP for Glamorgan in 1818 was something of a freak, a lawyer holding a county seat, but he was turned out in 1820 when the leading local gentry united against him. He was, by then, a local landowner himself and received support from lesser gentry there and from industrialists. He was chosen sheriff of Glamorgan in 1823–4 and the barrister William Vaughan of Llanelay made him his heir provided he took the name Vaughan, which he did in 1829.

John Edwards Vaughan was evidently anxious to return to parliament and from 1830 until 1832 he represented Wells, but he died in 1833 in the house he shared with John Nash in Regent Street. A year later John Lee Lee married his daughter, but she herself only survived the birth of their son, Vaughan Hanning Lee, in February 1836 by a few days. His second wife was the elder daughter of the 2nd Viscount Bridport.

The small, seventeenth-century farmhouse at Dillington had been altered by the Hannings; John Lee Lee, with the help of Nash's pupil James Pennethorne, transformed it in the 1830s into the Tudoresque mansion which still survives. The publisher Kegan Paul remembered 'the old house … in process of demolition, to make way for the new quasi-Elizabethan edifice, which would have been so much better had Mr Hanning-Lee [sic] waited but a few years longer, for the revival of architecture'. In the 1840s the improvements in the grounds were admired by Mr Lethbridge. Mr Lee, of course, served as a magistrate and a deputy lieutenant. He died in 1874, still in possession of a turquoise ring containing some of his first wife's hair.

Plans for rebuilding Dillington House; photograph by J. P. S. Dunning.

Vaughan Hanning Lee served in the Crimea and evidently enjoyed himself, hunting the local wild dogs as much as the Russian enemy as an officer in the Royal North British Fusiliers. His father several times had to pay debts accrued from drinking and gambling. Respectability arrived with the death in 1868 of his late mother's brother Nash Vaughan Edwards Vaughan, whose coal-producing estates he inherited and whose name Vaughan he took to become Vaughan Hanning Vaughan-Lee. He fully entered into the life of a Welsh landowner, becoming a major in the Glamorgan militia and serving as sheriff of the county in 1871–2, far more acceptable than his grandfather had been half a century earlier. On succeeding his father in 1874 he moved to Dillington, spent over £5500 on new stables, kennels and a laundry, and became MP for West Somerset, the seat he held until his death in 1882, and of course a magistrate and a deputy lieutenant. His two sons shared the family estate in 1882, the reason for an inventory of Dillington House which revealed twenty-four bedrooms in the main house and two in the butler's lodge, and in the

cellar 175 dozen bottles of claret, 87 dozen bottles of champagne, 72 of sherry and 64 of port.

Arthur Vaughan Hanning Vaughan-Lee succeeded to Dillington and Llanelay at the age of twenty while his brother John took Rheola and dropped the Lee from his surname. Arthur was a soldier who fought in the Boer War and retired with honour in 1911 as Colonel of the Royal Horse Guards (the Blues), MVO and holder of Orders from Prussia and Norway. He was a JP and a deputy lieutenant of the county. At the age of fifty-three he married the remarkable Mary Ursula Umfreville Pickering who still had a taste for fast cars in her eighties and at ninety was still shooting and fishing. Colonel Vaughan-Lee died in 1933; she died at the age of ninety-two, leaving Dillington to her daughter Elizabeth, wife of Major Allan Cameron. Their son Ewen manages the estate in trust for his children, lives in the house once occupied by John Hanning and, having been a prominent member of the Country Landowners' Association, now serves as Chairman of the Countryside Agency. He was sheriff of Somerset in 1986–7 and was appointed a deputy lieutenant in 1989. Dillington House has been leased to Somerset County Council since 1950.

Dillington House, Ilminster; Photograph by J. P. S. Dunning.

Waldegrave of Chewton

The Waldegraves, their name deriving from Walgrave in Northamptonshire, officially look back to the Suffolk man Sir Richard Waldegrave, speaker of the Commons in 1381–2, as the beginning of their significance. Geoffrey Noel Waldegrave, the 12th earl, speaking as President of the Somerset Archaeological and Natural History Society in 1970, apologised that his family, although granted the manor of Chewton in 1553, had not lived in the county until they were briefly at Harptree Court in the eighteenth century and not continuously until the 9th earl took up residence at Chewton Priory in 1898.

However, the family's connection with Somerset can be traced back to 1497 at Shurton in Stogursey and to 1529 at Spaxton where John Waldegrave, great-great-great grandson of Sir Richard, was found to be one of the heirs in the female line of John Hill (died 1434) and thus, genealogically speaking, descendant of Robert Fitchet, holder of estates in Somerset in 1166. Those estates in John Waldegrave's time included lands on and near the Quantocks but spreading to East Harptree and Radstock in the Mendips (the coal mines were later to make much money for the famous Countess Waldegrave) and further to Cornwall and Berkshire.

John's son Sir Edward died in the Tower of London in 1561. His sympathy for the catholic Princess Mary was not appreciated by the extreme protestants of Edward VI's government and he was only rescued from his first visit to the Tower by the princess's accession to the throne as Queen Mary. His reward was the manor of Chewton, membership of her Privy Council, and appointment as Master of the Great Wardrobe, but such a man was not appreciated by Queen Elizabeth.

Sir Edward's grandson, also Sir Edward, faithfully supported his king in the Civil War. In 1643 he was rewarded with a baronetcy and fought bravely at Saltash to keep the Parliamentarian Earl of Essex cooped up in Cornwall. He died in 1647 before the tragedy of his king's execution and long before the restoration of Charles II, which he would heartily have welcomed.

Lord Waldegrave spoke in his Presidential Address of the second rise of his family in the person of Cavalier Sir Edward's great grandson Henry, born in the year after the Restoration. What made him was his marriage in 1683 to Henrietta FitzJames, illegitimate daughter of James II by Arabella Churchill. 'For his pains', as Lord Waldegrave said, he was made Baron Waldegrave of Chewton early in 1686 and became a faithful servant to his king. In the few months when the king appointed catholics to political office, Lord Waldegrave was made Lord-Lieutenant of Somerset and recorder of Taunton. As Comptroller of the Royal Household he was intimately involved in the king's flight to France and died in James's service at St Germain in 1690, aged only twenty-eight.

James, Lord Waldegrave, first son and heir, was educated in France as a catholic but renounced his allegiance after his wife's death in 1719 and took his seat in the Lords in 1722. He was a Whig Lord of the Bedchamber to the first two Georges and a diplomat, for which, no doubt because he was 'mild and affable' and 'in high confidence with Sir Robert Walpole', he was in 1729 created Viscount Chewton and Earl Waldegrave. He sold at least some of his Somerset estates including Spaxton, Shurton and Raddington.

His son James moved in similar circles: a Lord of the Bedchamber to George II, Lord Warden of the Stannaries, Keeper of the Privy Purse to the Prince of Wales and his brother, and for four days in 1757 First Lord of the Treasury. Both he and his father were Knights of the Garter. When over forty he married Maria, an illegitimate granddaughter of Sir Robert Walpole, leaving on his death from smallpox in 1763 three daughters, the famous 'Three Ladies Waldegrave' painted by Sir Joshua Reynolds.

His brother and successor John was a soldier, leading a brigade at the battle of Minden in 1759, later becoming a general and holding offices at Court. He was extremely thin; Horace Walpole, his wife's uncle, described how he was shot through his hat and his coat and would have been shot through his body 'if he had any'. The President Earl described him and his son George (died 1789) as 'sound but fairly undistinguished'. The 5th earl was drowned at the age of ten at Eton in 1794; the 6th, Lord Waldegrave said, 'we won't speak of' a soldier who eventually married his mistress.

George Edward, the 6th earl's eldest legitimate son, married Frances Elizabeth Anne, widow of his eldest brother (legal because married in Scotland) and the daughter of an opera singer of Jewish descent. Frances was a remarkable woman. On the death from drink of George Edward in 1846 she married thirdly George Granville Vernon-Harcourt and finally, in 1863, Chichester Samuel Parkinson-Fortescue, created in 1874 Baron Carlingford. After 1846 she continued to call herself Countess Waldegrave and somehow kept hold of the Waldegrave estates and other family possessions. In 1876 the estates amounted to over 11,000 acres, mostly in Somerset and Essex but also around her home at Strawberry Hill, Twickenham, worth together £17,771.

William Waldegrave, uncle and successor of the last earl, was a naval officer. His son tried the navy, Cambridge, and farming in Canada but found his home in the army where, at the age of thirty-eight and while his father was still alive, he died at Scutari of wounds received at the battle of the Alma. So the 8th earl was succeeded by his grandson William Frederick, a soldier and Conservative politician, perhaps suitably Captain of the Yeomen of the Guard 1896–1905.

Geoffrey Noel, the 12th earl, became Viscount Chewton on the death of the invalid 10th earl in 1933 when his father, a retired parish priest aged nearly eighty, succeeded to the family title. At Chewton Mendip he built up a flourishing home farm where Cheddar cheese was produced in the stables, all that he sensibly preserved of Countess Waldegrave's extravagant Chewton Priory. He served as Joint Parliamentary Secretary at the Ministry of Agriculture, Fisheries and Food 1958–62 after distinguished service for

William Frederick Waldegrave, 9th Earl Waldegrave (died 1930).

Mates

agriculture in the West of England and was successively Chairman of the Forestry Commission and Lord Warden of the Stannaries between 1963 and 1976. Locally he served for more than twenty years on Somerset County Council and was a member and trustee of the Somerset Archaeological Society from 1939. Among many other achievements was his successful chairmanship of the Wells Cathedral Appeal. He was made KG in 1971 and GCVO in 1976.

James Sherbrooke Waldegrave, his successor in 1995, has for some years run the family farms. His brother William, a former president of the Oxford Union and Fellow of All Souls, Oxford, was Conservative MP for Bristol (West) 1979–97 and a government minister.

Wills

Henry Overton Wills was born in Salisbury in 1761, the son of a jeweller and watchmaker, and had arrived in Bristol by 1786 when he became a partner in Wills, Watkins and Co., tobacconists. He evidently provided the capital and Watkins the expertise, but in 1790 his was the only name in the business, which in 1791 moved from the city centre in Castle Street to a site historically in Somerset, in Redcliffe Street. He and his wife, the former Ann Day, moved to a house not far away in Redcliffe Hill in 1808, so they were by then Somerset residents by historical extension. A century later the county had become actually their home; in 1906 Willses were living at Dulverton, Clevedon, Blagdon, Wrington and Kelston. They took the county to their hearts and served it well.

Rebecca Overton, Henry's mother, was the daughter of a leading Andover Congregationalist, and the Wills family became influential members of the Penn Street Tabernacle, joining Bristol's nonconformist industrial and commercial élite, and the business prospered. In 1805, with a capital of about £5000, sales were worth £16,500; in 1808 £28,000. Ten years later Wills salesmen were regularly riding a huge area stretching between Cornwall and Cheshire. H.O. Wills died in 1826.

H. O. Wills (died 1826).
B. W. E. Alford, *W.D. and H.O. Wills...1786-1965* (1973)

The history of the Wills family is, of course, the history of the firm and of Bristol's tobacco industry; it is also in great measure the history of Bristol University. Henry Overton Wills had two remarkable sons who left issue: William Day (1797–1865), one of whose two sons, William Henry, of Coombe Lodge, became Lord Winterstoke and died in 1911; and a second Henry Overton (1800–1871). A third Henry Overton (1828–1911), son of the second, lived at Kelston Knoll, Newbridge Hill, near Bath, and was eldest brother to Edward Payson, created a baronet in 1904, and living for a time in Clevedon; and Frederick, of Northmoor, Dulverton, created a baronet in 1897, MP for North Bristol 1900–6. Henry Overton was virtual creator of Bristol University by his generous donation of £100,000 to University College on condition that it applied for a charter and with it university status. It was only right that he should be its first chancellor.

Sir G. A. Wills (died 1928).
B. W. E. Alford, *W.D. and H.O. Wills...1786-1965* (1973)

Sir John Wills, Lord-Lieutenant of Avon 1974-96 and of Somerset 1994-8.
Bath Chronicle

In the next generation Frederick's second son, Gilbert Alan Hamilton Wills, was in a busy career a Unionist MP for Taunton and later for Weston super Mare, chairman of the Imperial Tobacco Co. and a director of the Great Western Railway Co., and was created Baron Dulverton in 1929 in recognition of political and public service in his birthplace. George Alfred Wills (1854–1928), eldest son of H.O., was like his father intimately concerned with the university and was made a baronet in 1923. His brother Henry Herbert Wills (1856–1922) lived at Barleywood, Wrington, and was a Somerset magistrate and county alderman. Walter Melville Wills, the third brother, lived on the Somerset side of the Avon Gorge at Leigh Woods. In 1913 George and Henry gave the university £150,000 in memory of their father, from which in due time came Sir George Oatley's Wills Memorial Building, and Walter gave £20,000 as an endowment.

In the next generation Wills business acumen and Wills public service continued unabated. Walter Douglas Melville Wills, who had bought Barleywood from his uncle in 1921, was a captain in the North Somerset Yeomanry, a Somerset county councillor from 1925 to 1940, a county alderman 1940– 48 and a magistrate from 1927. He was sheriff in 1946. In the next generation came John Vernon Wills, TD, KCVO, succeeding as the 4th baronet when his brother Peter was killed in North Italy in 1944. Sir John, of Langford Court, served with the Coldstream Guards in Malaya and was on the board of several important Bristol companies but gave time for public service as magistrate and Somerset county councillor, as sheriff in 1968–9, as Pro-Chancellor of Bath University from 1979, as the first and only Lord-Lieutenant of Avon 1974–96 and as Lord-Lieutenant of Somerset from 1994 until his sudden death in 1998. His son David James Vernon Wills succeeded as the 5th baronet and to an amazing family tradition.

Wyndham of Orchard

The Wyndhams began dangerously, or rather their rise was fraught with some danger, for it began when York and Lancaster took sides and in Norfolk, the county of so much political chicanery. The family name probably derives from the Norfolk market town near which John Wyndham (which he then spelled Wymondham), but evidently a native of Norwich, held land by 1436. In about 1450 he bought what was called the reversion of a much more prestigious estate in the north of the county, held until his death in 1442 by Sir Simon Felbrigg, the last of a distinguished line. John Wyndham, anxious to move in, upset not only distant members of the Felbrigg family but also the villagers on the estate. In his absence from his new home his wife was dragged away by her hair. Wyndham threatened force but finally established his right by a judicious distribution of cash. John's son John succeeded in 1475 when both father and son had forsaken Lancaster for York and, fighting for Henry VII at the battle of Stoke, was knighted; but his relations, and more especially his stepson-in-law the former Duke of Suffolk, was too dangerous to know. In 1502 Wyndham and Sir James Tyrell, probably murderer of the princes in the Tower, were executed just outside that same Tower for treason.

Thanks to kinship with the Howards, Dukes of Norfolk, Sir John Wyndham's disgrace was reversed as his elder son Thomas made his mark as a naval commander and a member of the king's council. By the time of his death in 1522 Vice-Admiral Thomas had already arranged for the marriage of one of his daughters, Margaret, to Andrew, son of Sir Hugh Luttrell of Dunster. A few years later that Somerset-Norfolk connection was strengthened when Thomas's second son John, having spent some time at the French court in the retinue of Princess Mary, sister of Henry VIII and Queen of France, met and married Elizabeth, the heiress of one of the several branches of the Sydenhams, whose home was at Orchard outside Williton.

John Wyndham was knighted at the coronation of Edward VI in 1547 and may have served in such military capacity as his birth and connections required, but the contents of his house at Orchard, as expressed in his will, suggests a man rather more attuned to the gentle life of his youth. He died

in 1574, four years after his eldest son, and his estates descended to his grandson, also John, whose birth was something of a miracle, since his pregnant mother had been assumed dead and was lying overnight in St Decuman's church ready for burial. The parish sexton, trying to cut a ring from her finger as she lay in her coffin, found to his alarm that his crude efforts at surgery had revived the lady. The young heir to Orchard, connected through his mother with the Wadhams, himself married a Portman; the Norfolk family was thus thoroughly enmeshed among the Somerset gentry, but on the death of his nephew Thomas Wyndham of Felbrigg he also found himself owner of the Norfolk lands of the family.

Sir John Wyndham, as he inevitably became, seems to have had more concern for personal interests – presumably including his considerable estate – than for public service, though the fact that one of the royalist Wyndham cousins of Kentsford should have removed goods to the value of £4000 from his home at Orchard might suggest personal sympathy with the other side like his nephew William Portman. He himself was well over eighty when the Civil War broke out and he died in 1645. John, his son and heir, was married to the daughter of the royalist Sir Ralph Hopton, and his death in 1649 probably saved Orchard from financial punishment, and the heir, William Wyndham, was of a more compromising nature than his cousins. He accepted a baronetcy from Cromwell and sat in parliament for Taunton in 1659; yet Charles II accepted him as a loyal subject and he died still a baronet in 1683.

Another William Wyndham succeeded his father Edward in 1695 at the age of ten. He was a natural politician, entering parliament in 1710 for the county of Somerset and remained a member for the county until his death in 1740. His marriage to a daughter of the Whig Duke of Somerset did him no harm; his friendship with Henry St John, Viscount Bolingbroke, put him among the leaders of the Tory government. His first appointment was as Master of the Queen's Hart and Buckhounds (which cost him money), but soon he became Secretary at War, in which post he made sensible reductions in the army now that peace with France had been signed. Neither the peace nor the trade arrangements that went with it found favour with the Whig opposition, but Sir William himself continued in political favour, becoming Chancellor and Under-Treasurer of the Exchequer, and soon afterwards a Privy Councillor. His power lasted little more than a year, for the death of Queen Anne in August 1714 sent him into the political wilderness for the rest of his life. Those who thought him far too friendly towards France were later happy to discover at Orchard evidence of a Jacobite conspiracy, though Sir William had thought better of an uprising in Somerset. Nevertheless, imprisonment in the Tower for a few months was perhaps lenient. Thereafter, Sir William headed the Tory opposition to the Whig Sir Robert Walpole in the House of Commons. A contemporary said he was 'the most made for a great man' that ever he knew.

Sir William died in 1740 and was followed by his son Charles, a Tory like himself and MP successively for Bridgwater, Appleby and Taunton until 1750 when he succeeded to the titles of Earl of Egremont and Baron Cockermouth inherited from his uncle the Duke of Somerset along with estates all over England and a principal residence at Petworth. Cumberland and Sussex became the chief areas of his interest and his main

Above left: Monumental brass to Sir John Wyndham (died 1574), St Decuman's church, Watchet.

A. B. Connor, *Monumental Brasses in Somerset* (1970), plate lxxxviii

Above right: Monumental brass to John Wyndham (died 1572), St Decuman's church, Watchet.

A. B. Connor, *Monumental Brasses in Somerset* (1970), plate lxxxix

personal characteristic was the pride inherited from his grandfather. His son George had six illegitimate children, of whom two sons inherited the Sussex and Cumberland estates while to his nephew, also George, passed the titles and the Somerset and Devon holdings in 1837. He died without children in 1860 when the titles became extinct; his widow lived on at Orchard until her own death in 1876.

William Wyndham of the Dinton branch of the family which had originated way back in the seventeenth century with Sir John Wyndham's youngest son, the judge Sir Wadham, now succeeded to Orchard and the Devon land. He died in 1914 and his son, also William, sold the Wiltshire estates two years later, thereafter making Orchard his home and Somerset the field of his educational endeavours. M.R. James, the provost of Eton, visited Orchard in 1930 and recorded 'a strange household – stout and bearded William, who repeats the beginnings of his sentences twice or thrice. Old Mother Wyndham, thin and deaf and silent. Three Misses Wyndham of mature age'. Stout and bearded William may have been, but enormously generous to the county museum and to Somerset schoolchildren, whose successors still benefit from his benefactions in support of local history.

Such public generosity was poorly rewarded. Duty payable on William Wyndham's death in 1950 forced the sale of much land, but the new owner of Orchard, William's nephew George, abandoned a diplomatic career and threw himself into the role of local public servant. He was a deputy lieutenant, and a member of Somerset County Council from 1949 to 1980, serving for two periods as vice-chairman and as chairman 1969–74. He died in 1982 leaving in a daughter Katherine an historian with a deep understanding of her ancestry and passionately concerned with the survival of her family home and its immediate estate.

William Wyndham (died 1950), aged 21; photograph by Lafayette.

SAS

155

Envoi

Opposite: *Combe Sydenham, woodcut by Rachel Reckitt.*

H. Bishop, *Rachel Reckitt* (2001)

In the medieval centuries families had come to settle in Somerset, broadly speaking, for dynastic reasons, joining in marriage with the relatively few native famiIes of similar status. From the Later Middle Ages Somerset was beginning to attract a new breed of entrepreneur, drawn either by the natural riches of the land or the commercial possibilities of its geography. Still, land remained the only secure investment, and a fashionable home on that land was a sign of social acceptance. Titles were relatively few in a county of such independence of mind, peerages even fewer (it was on the whole safer that way in times of political upheaval), though the name Somerset was proudly borne by families whose more regular place of residence was outside but who were yet anxious to retain even the smallest link.

Commercial entrepreneurs of more modern times easily turned from trade to banking or expanded their trade to embrace the wider possibilities of their raw materials, but often the country house was substituted for something more modest and in an almost urban setting. The railways which had so effectively widened the markets of those entrepreneurs opened their county to businessmen and their families on holiday. They came for recreation, not to invest, not to marry, not to make money; they came attracted by the countryside and with the leisure to enjoy it. Thus came the architect Frank Norman Reckitt, grandson of the founder of one of Hull's successful businesses, and his artist wife Beatrice. They came regularly from about 1900 and they settled in 1922. Relatives followed them, grandchildren came on holidays. In a century they have become fixtures, even if they found themselves for a time in other parts of the world. The names Golsoncott and Reckitt have become synonymous, the permanent home of the artist Rachel Reckitt, the childhood holiday home of her niece Penelope Lively, and still (albeit a more modest building) a family retreat. That part of West Somerset which has in different ways inspired the creativity of grandmother, aunt and niece is the land which attracted the Mohuns and the Luttrells for different reasons and in a different age. All three are Somerset families.

Acknowledgements

The works listed in the bibliography are sufficient evidence that this book could not have been written without the help of many people, but particular thanks are offered to my colleague Mary Siraut, Assistant Editor of the Victoria History of Somerset, whose work on the Clark and Trevelyan families in particular has been invaluable; to David Bromwich, who has made the task of choosing illustrations so much easier than it might have been; to Colin Brett, from whom I have taken information about the early Horners in advance of publication; to Mrs Sophie Rawlins, who gave me information from the diary of her father Prebendary Bates-Harbin; and to Di Stanton, who has so readily answered my questions about the Lieutenancy. (Lady Gass, Mr Peter Speke and Mr Simon Heneage have provided pictures from their family archives; owners of other illustrations are acknowledged in the picture credits.)

Steven Pugsley asked me to write this book; I hope it is what he wanted. My wife Anne has generously borne the pressures which it has occasioned; it is almost as much hers as mine.

Abbreviations used in image credits:
SAS – Somerset Archaeological Society
SASP – SAS Proceedings
SCC – Somerset County Council
Mates – *Mates County Series, Somerset, Historical, Descriptive, Biographical* (1908)
Lodge – E. Lodge, *Portraits of Illustrious Personages* (12 vols. 1835)

Bibliography

GENERAL

Burke's Peerage and Baronetage (various editions)

Burke's Landed Gentry (various editions)

Complete Peerage (14 volumes, 1910–59)

History of Parliament (23 volumes, 1964–92 continuing)

Victoria History of Somerset, ed. R.W. Dunning, iii–vii (1974–99)

D. Cannadine, *The Decline and Fall of the British Aristocracy* (1990)

J. Collinson, *History of the County of Somerset* (1791)

R.W. Dunning, *Some Somerset Country Houses, a personal selection* (1991)

S.W. Rawlins (as S.W. Bates Harbin), *Members of Parliament for the County of Somerset* (1939); *The Sheriffs of Somerset* (1968)

D. Underdown, *Somerset in the Civil War and Interregnum* (1973)

J.C. Wedgewood (and A. Holt), *History of Parliament, Biographies, 1439–1509* (1936)

I.J. Sanders, *English Baronies* (1963)

FAMILY SPECIFIC

Acland-Hood: S. Keynes, 'The discovery and first publication of the Alfred Jewel', *Somerset Archaeology and Natural History*, cxxxvi (1992), 1–8

Beaufort: M.K. Jones and M.G. Underwood, *The King's Mother* (1992)

Cely-Trevilian: M. Siraut (ed.), *The Trevelyan Letters to 1840* (Somerset Record Soc. lxxx (1990))

Clark: *Quaker Inheritance, 1871–1961: A Portrait of Roger Clark of Street* (1970); P. Lovell (ed.), *Somerset Anthology* (twenty-four pieces by Roger Clark of Street, 1871–1961) (1975)

Dickinson: J. Burden, *Winging Westward* (1974)

Fox: G. Allen, *Yesterday's Town: Wellington* (1987); H. Fox, *Quaker Homespun* (1958); M. Hagen and M.P. Fox, *More Than Two Hundred Years: Wellington and the Foxes* (2000)

Elton: M. Elton, *The Annals of the Elton Family* (1994)

Envoi: Penelope Lively, *A House Unlocked* (2001); H. Bishop, *Rachel Reckitt* (2001)

Gibbs: W.M. Mathew, *The House of Gibbs and the Peruvian Guano Monopoly* (Royal Historical Soc. 1981)

Harbin: S.W. Rawlins, 'Newton Surmaville', *Proceedings of Somerset*

Archaeological and Natural History Society, cix (1964/5), 30–5

Helyar: *A Short Account of Coker Court and Its Owners* (n.d.)

Hippisley: I. Fitzroy Jones (edited and extended), *Some Notes on the Hippisley Family*, collected by Alfred E. Hippisley (privately printed 1952)

Hobhouse: H. Hobhouse, *Hobhouse Memoirs* (1927)

Leir: M. McGarvie, 'The Priory, Ditcheat, Somerset' in *Trans. Ancient Monuments Soc.* new series 24 (1979–80), 75–125

Luttrell: H.M. Binding, *Discovering Dunster* (n.d.); H.C. Maxwell Lyte, *A History of Dunster* (1909)

Lyte: H.C. Maxwell Lyte, *The Lytes of Lytes Cary* (1895)

Mohun: H.C. Maxwell Lyte, *A History of Dunster* (1909)

Phelips: R.S. More, 'The Records of Virtue: Gentility in Early Modern England', Ph.D. thesis, Brown University, U.S.A. (1998)

Poulett: C.G. Winn, *The Pouletts of Hinton St George* (revised edition 1995)

Smyth: J. Bettey, *Calendar of the Correspondence of the Smyth Family of Ashton Court, 1548–1642* (Bristol Record Soc. 1982)

Stawell: G.D. Stawell, *A Quantock Family* (1910)

Stuckey: M. Churchman, 'The Stuckeys of Somerset' (typescript in Somerset Studies Libr., Taunton); R. Dunning, 'Nineteenth-Century Parochial Sources' in *Studies in Church History* 11 (1975), 301–8

Trevelyan: R.J.E. Bush and G.U.S. Corbett, 'Nettlecombe Court' (*Field Studies*, 3, no. 2 (1970)), 275–96; M. Siraut (ed.), *The Trevelyan Letters to 1840* (Somerset Record Soc. lxxx (1990))

Vaughan-Lee: C. Kegan Paul, *Memories* (1899, repr. 1971); N. Smith, *The Story of Dillington: A Thousand Years* (2000)

Wills: B.W. Alford, *W.D. & H.O. Wills and the Development of the U.K. Tobacco Industry, 1786–1965* (1973); B. Cottle and J. Sherborne, *The Life of a University* (1951)

Wyndham: H.A. Wyndham, *A Family History 1410–1688: the Wyndhams of Norfolk and Somerset* (1939); *A Family History 1688–1837): the Wyndhams of Somerset, Sussex and Wiltshire* (1950); M. Cox, *M.R. James* (1986)